fun & funky crochet

fun & funky crochet

30 EXCITING PROJECTS FOR A STYLISH NEW LOOK

Sophie Britten

Martingale®
& COMPANY

Copyright © Collins & Brown Limited, 2005

An imprint of **Chrysalis** Books Group plc

Text © Sophie Britten 2005

The right of Sophie Britten to be identified as the author of this work has been asserted by her in accordance with the Copyright, Designs and Patents Act, 1988.

Martingale®
& C O M P A N Y

Martingale & Company
20205 144th Avenue NE
Woodinville, WA 98072-8478 USA
www.martingale-pub.com

Reproduction by Mission Productions, Hong Kong
Printed and bound by SNP Leefung, China
10 09 08 07 06 05   8 7 6 5 4 3 2

Library of Congress Cataloging-in-Publication data is available upon request.
ISBN 1-56477-619-0

Mission Statement
Dedicated to providing quality products and service to inspire creativity.

Designed by Lotte Oldfield
Edited and pattern checked by Susan Huran and Janet Rehfeldt
Indexed by Isobel McLean

contents

introduction

Crochet is one of the most versatile and rewarding crafts. Although there is some dispute, it is widely believed that the craft originated in France. The modern name derives directly from the old French word *croché,* meaning hook. It is thought that crochet was practiced in the eighteenth century by French nuns, who took their craft to Ireland where it quickly became popular, especially for making the lace with which Irish crochet is now synonymous.

Not just for nuns, crochet is now more popular than ever before. Today's crochet is a far cry from the frilly doilies and lacy collars that were fashionable right up until the Victorian times. Crochet is young and fun, and it has never been easier to do. *Fun and Funky Crochet* features over 25 patterns for unique clothes and accessories, plus loads of ideas for customizing your jackets, sweaters and jeans. It also includes the basic techniques and incorporates many of the traditional elements of the craft, while giving the projects a new twist to bring crochet right up to the minute.

It's easy to make original clothes and accessories. Crochet is marvelously versatile, for shaping or using textured stitches like bobbles, loops, or ripples. There are lots of different ways you can customize your clothes with crochet, giving a new funky look to an old garment. A beginner can start creating almost straight away. Once you learn the basics and a few stitches, the possibilities are endless. Add flowers, motifs, patches, edges, cuffs, and collars, or simply crochet a design right onto your clothes. The book also explains how you can add beads and baubles (or anything that can be threaded onto the yarn) to make beaded edgings.

You don't have to be a designer or an expert to make these amazing things—all you need is a crochet hook and some yarn. So let *Fun and Funky Crochet* inspire you to learn this simple but beautiful craft.

fantastic yarns

You can crochet with practically anything that has length and flexibility. If you had a large enough hook, and a big emergency, you could even crochet your bedsheets together.

But before you go that far, there are some truly fantastic yarns around that are just waiting to be picked up and turned into amazing creations.

Most crochet suppliers sell cotton crochet yarns, which are principally for lace-making, and also a range of Goldfingering or metallic thread and yarn, which is a synthetic yarn woven though with metallic thread. It comes in a wide variety of colors, and I always make sure I have some gold or silver on hand for sparkly trims on hats, crewnecks, cardigans—anything and everything.

You can also crochet with any knitting yarns that are available in your local yarn shop or craft store. As well as the traditional natural fibers such as wool and cotton, there are some really exciting mixed synthetic-and-natural and totally synthetic yarns. Recent years have seen a proliferation in multicolored, bobbled, textured, spangly, and otherwise exotic yarns. And in general, one ball is enough to make over an item of clothing or make a small accessory, such as a bag or hat. Still it never hurts to buy more than you think you'll need—most shops will exchange or refund what you don't use.

If you can't find what you're looking for in the shops, take a look online at some of the many shops or wholesalers selling all kinds of wools, synthetic yarns, ribbons, metallics, and a wide choice of beautiful and hard-to-find natural wools, such as mohair. (For a list of suppliers, see the back of the book). If you're just planning small projects, some discount or outlet stores sell bags of odds and discontinued ends of stock very cheaply.

tips & hints

Dye lots:
When buying more than one ball of a particular yarn, make sure the dye lot numbers printed on the ball band are the same; otherwise, there may be a slight variation in color.

Hook size:
Most yarn manufacturers will tell you on the ball band what size *knitting* needle they recommend you use; for crochet, you should use half a size or a whole size larger. The larger the hook, the larger the stitch and the looser your work will be.

Choosing yarns:
To ensure your crocheted article appears the same as in the pattern, you should use the yarn that is recommended. If you cannot find the same yarn, choose one of a similar weight and type and crochet a sample to check the gauge and appearance.

Washing instructions:
Care instructions should be given on the ball band; however, where there are none or you are unsure, you should wash a sample first.

materials

Unlike many other crafts, crochet uses amazingly few materials. All you need to get started is some yarn and a crochet hook, although there are a few other items that will come in handy.

Tapestry needles:
These are large blunt needles that are used for joining seams together.

Tape measure:
A tape measure is indispensable for checking gauge and when making fitted garments, as you will often need to measure the work.

Scissors:
Scissors should be small and sharp for cutting yarn.

Crochet hook conversion chart:
Normal crochet hooks vary in size from 2 mm to 15 mm and are 6 inches (15 cm) long. They are most commonly available in plastic and aluminum. The larger hooks will be plastic as this is lighter and easier to hold. You may have also come across steel hooks. These tend to be much smaller (less than 2 mm) and are used for intricate lace-making and filet work.

You may find that different pattern books use different systems to express sizes. The chart on the right will help you choose the correct hook.

METRIC SIZES (mm)	US SIZES	UK/CANADIAN SIZES
2.0	–	14
2.25	B/1	13
2.5	–	12
2.75	C/2	–
3.0	–	11
3.25	D/3	10
3.5	E/4	9
3.75	F/5	–
4.0	G/6	8
4.5	7	7
5.0	H/8	6
5.5	I/9	5
6.0	J/10	4
6.5	K/10½	3
7.0	–	2
8.0	L/11	0
9.0	M/13	00
10.0	N/15	000

following instructions

Crochet patterns use special terminology that is often abbreviated or shown as symbols on a chart. Becoming familiar with these will make your crocheting quicker and more enjoyable.

Before you start on any project, read through the instructions to make sure you understand all of the information. Where different sizes are given, clearly mark which size you are going to make and highlight instructions for that size throughout the pattern. This will make it much easier to follow.

Where there is a recurring instruction, the start of the section of the pattern to be repeated is indicated with an asterisk. For example: *dc, ch 2, dc in ch-2 sp; rep from * until last st.

Abbreviations

The table of abbreviations (right) lists the most common abbreviations and all those that are used in this book. However, it is not an exhaustive list as there are many different crochet stitches, not all of which are used in this book.

beg	Beginning
BL	Back loop
BLO	Back loop only
ch	Chain
ch sp	Chain space
cont	Continue
dc	Double crochet
dec	Decrease
dtr	Double treble
fl	Front loop
FLO	Front loop only
foll	Following
inc	Increase
patt	Pattern
rem	Remaining
rep	Repeat
RS	Right side
sc	Single crochet
sp	Space
sl st	Slip stitch
st(s)	Stitch(es)
tch	Turning chain
tog	Together
tr	Triple crochet
trtr	Triple treble
WS	Wrong side
yo	Yarn over

Charts

A chart is often used in filet crochet. It is based on a square grid, in which vertical lines represent double crochet stitches and horizontal lines represent chains. Patterns are created by filling in some of the squares; where a square is filled with a dot, a chain is replaced by a double crochet.

Charts can also be used to give directions for color patterns.

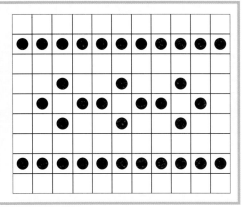

Gauge

This is the number of rows and stitches per centimeter or inch, usually measured over 4 square inches (10 cm). The gauge will determine the size of the finished item. The correct gauge is given at the beginning of each pattern. Crochet a small swatch using the recommended yarn and hook to make sure you are working to the correct gauge. If your work is too loose, choose a hook that is one size smaller, and if it is too tight, choose a hook the next size up. When making clothes, it is important to check your gauge before you start; it is not worth making something the wrong size. When measuring work, lay it on a flat surface and always measure at the center, rather than the side edges.

The good news is that few of the patterns in this book require you to work to an exact gauge. However, it is important to be consistent in order to make a nice, even fabric that is neither too tight nor too loose. The advantage of working with fluffy,

furry, and other textured yarns is that minor inconsistencies won't show.

To keep your gauge even, it is a good idea to have a piece of scrap crochet on hand to warm up with each time you pick up your work.

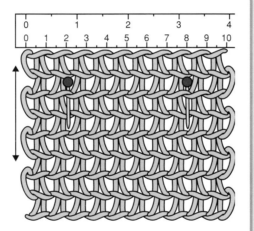

tips & hints

- If you are making a large number of base chains, it is worth leaving a long tail when you start so that if you find on your first row that you haven't done enough chains, you can undo the slip knot and create a few more. Similarly, don't worry if you have done too many chains, as these can usually be unworked and woven in at the end.

- Always finish the row or round you are working on to avoid losing your place in the pattern.

- Unless the pattern says otherwise, always join a new ball of yarn at the end of a row, not in the middle. This way it can be neatly woven in afterward.

- Always turn the work clockwise to avoid twisting your stitches.

learning to crochet

Crochet is a relatively simple and hugely rewarding way of making clothes, accessories, and household items with wonderful textures.

Crochet is made up of a series of interlocking loops. Unlike knitting, each stitch is completed before working the next, so after each stitch you are left with only one loop of yarn on your hook. The advantage of working one complete stitch at a time is that you avoid the risk of dropping stitches.

Crochet is easy to learn and once you have mastered the basics, you will be able to make a wide variety of wonderful items.

First you will need a crochet hook: a 4 or 5 mm one is a good choice for beginners. As for yarns, it will be easier to see what you are doing if you use a smooth yarn, so avoid working with any yarns that are too fluffy (like mohair) until you become more confident.

Holding the hook

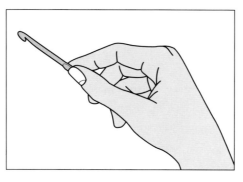

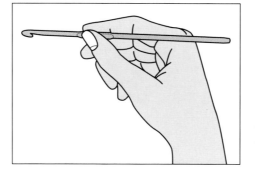

If you are right-handed, hold the hook like a knife in your right hand (see above top). You can also hold the hook like a pencil (see above) if you find that more comfortable.

Controlling your yarn

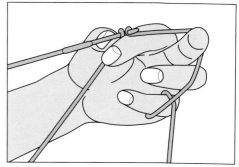

Wrap the yarn around your little finger and over the third, second, and index fingers as shown. Extend the second/middle finger to control the yarn and hold the work firmly between the thumb and index finger.

If you are left-handed, you should hold the hook in your left hand and the yarn in your right. Reverse the instructions. It may be helpful to prop up the book in front of a mirror.

Getting started

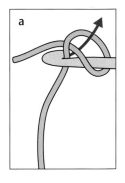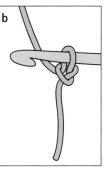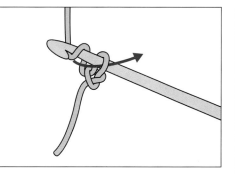

Start off by making a slipknot: make a loop near the end of the yarn; then insert the hook into the loop from front to back and draw another loop through it (a). Pull the knot close to the hook but not too tight (b).

Now you are ready to crochet. Most crochet starts with a base chain, which is a series of chain stitches.

To make a chain (ch), wrap the yarn around the hook from back to front (this is called a yarn over, or yo) and draw it through the loop on the hook (above left). This makes 1 chain stitch.

If you are completely new to crochet, practice making chains until you have a smooth action and can easily make even chains of the same size.

basic stitches

Start by making a series of chains—around 10 will be enough. Now you're ready to practice the following stitches.

Slip stitch (sl st)

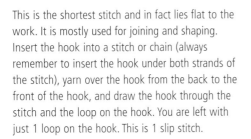

This is the shortest stitch and in fact lies flat to the work. It is mostly used for joining and shaping. Insert the hook into a stitch or chain (always remember to insert the hook under both strands of the stitch), yarn over the hook from the back to the front of the hook, and draw the hook through the stitch and the loop on the hook. You are left with just 1 loop on the hook. This is 1 slip stitch.

Single crochet (sc)

This is the most common and shortest fabric-making stitch. It creates a compact fabric that is worked forward and backward in rows.

Insert the hook into the second chain from the hook, yarn over the hook, draw the loop through your work (a), yarn over and draw the hook through both loops on the hook (b). You are left with 1 loop on the hook. This is 1 single crochet. Repeat into the next stitch or chain. Work until all chains or stitches are worked into. This is 1 row of single crochet. At the end of the row, make 1 chain stitch—this is your turning chain—turn the work and work 1 single crochet into each stitch of the previous row, ensuring you insert the hook under both loops of the stitch you are crocheting into.

Half double crochet (hdc)

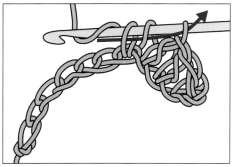

This stitch is similar to single crochet, but taller. Yarn over the hook before inserting the hook into the third chain from the hook, yarn over, draw 1 loop through the work, yarn over, draw through all 3 loops on the hook, leaving just 1 loop on the hook. This is 1 half double crochet.

When you reach the end of the row, make 2 chains—this counts as the first stitch of the next row. Turn the work, skip the first half double crochet of the previous row, and insert the hook into the second stitch of the new row. Continue to work until the end of the row. At the end of the row, work the last half double into the top of the turning chain of the row below.

Double crochet (dc)

This stitch is taller yet. As with the half double crochet, start by wrapping the yarn over the hook and insert the hook into the fourth chain from the hook, yarn over, draw 1 loop through the work (a), yarn over, draw through the first 2 loops on the hook, yarn over, draw through the remaining 2 loops on the hook (b), leaving just 1 loop on the hook. This is 1 double crochet.

When you reach the end of the row, make 3 chains. These count as the first stitch of the next row. Turn the work and skip the first double crochet of the previous row; insert the hook into the second stitch of the new row. Continue to work until the end of the row, inserting the last double crochet into the top of the turning chain of the row below.

basic techniques

As well as working from right to left in rows, crochet can also be worked circular (referred to as working in the round), or even in a continuous spiral to make seamless items such as hats, bags, and other rounded objects.

Making fabric—working in rows

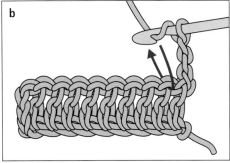

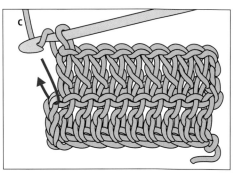

To make a flat fabric in crochet, as with knitting, you work back and forth in rows. First make as many chain stitches as you require. This row is called the base chain. To allow for the height of the stitch, insert the hook into the second chain from the hook (not counting the chain on the hook) for single crochet, third chain from the hook for double crochet, and so on.

Work from right to left, inserting the hook under 2 of the 3 threads in each chain.

When you reach the end of the row, you need to work a turning chain. This is one or more chains, depending on the height of the stitch. Turning chains should be worked as follows:

Single crochet: 1 chain
Half double: 2 chains
Double: 3 chains
Triple: 4 chains
Double treble: 5 chains

Now turn the work to begin working on the next row (remember always to turn your work in the same direction). When working in single crochet, insert the hook into the first stitch in the new row and work each stitch to the end of the row, excluding the turning chain. For all other stitches, unless the pattern states otherwise, the turning chain counts as the first stitch, skip 1 stitch (b) and work each stitch to the end of the row, including the top of the turning chain (c).

Making fabric—working in the round

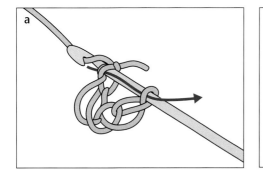

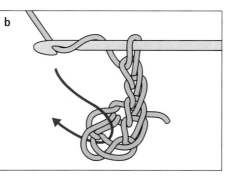

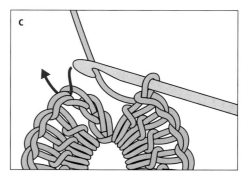

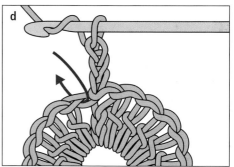

Crochet in the round starts with a ring. To make a ring, make a series of chains and join the last chain to the first with a slip stitch (a). To make the first round, work a starting chain to the height of the stitch you are working in (for example, single crochet—1 chain, double crochet—3 chains). Then work as many stitches as you need into the center of the ring (b) and finish the round with a slip stitch into the first stitch (c).

Begin the second and subsequent rounds with a starting chain. Then insert the hook under the top 2 loops of each stitch in the previous round (d). At the end of the round, join to the top of the starting chain with a slip stitch.

Changing colors

Increasing

Bobble

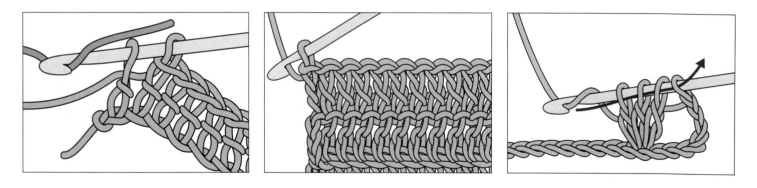

The patterns in this book will only require you to change color at the end of the row or round. To do this, change yarns during the last stitch in the row by working the last 2 loops of the stitch off the hook using the new yarn so that the new color is ready to be used for the turning chain. If you are going to use the original color again in a few rows, don't cut the yarn, but carry it up the side or the back if you are working in rounds.

As with knitting, fabric is often shaped by increasing the number of stitches in a row or round. To increase, simply work an additional stitch into the next stitch. A single increase is made by working 2 stitches into the same stitch. You can of course increase by more than 1 stitch at a time.

This method of working several stitches in the same place can also be used to create interesting textures such as bobbles, which are 2 or more stitches worked into the same stitch and joined together at the top.

Leaving the last loop of each stitch unworked, work specified number of stitches into the same stitch, in this instance 3 double crochet stitches, yarn over, draw yarn through all 4 loops on the hook.

Decreasing

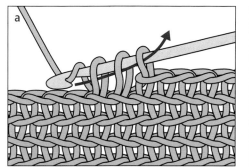  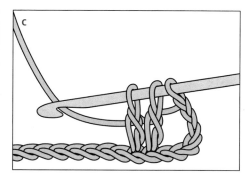

Fabric can also be shaped by decreasing the number of stitches in a row or round. To decrease, 2 or more stitches are worked together.

sc2tog

To decrease 1 stitch in single crochet (sc2tog), insert hook into the next stitch, yarn over, draw through the work, insert hook into the next stitch, yarn over, draw through the work, yarn over, draw through all 3 loops, leaving just 1 loop.

sc3tog

To decrease by 2 stitches in single crochet, work 3 stitches together (sc3tog) by working as for sc2tog until you have 3 loops on the hook, insert the hook into the next stitch, yarn over, draw through the work, yarn over and draw through all 4 loops.

dc2tog

To decrease 1 stitch in double crochet (dc2tog), yarn over, insert hook into the next stitch, yarn over, draw through the work, yarn over, draw through 2 loops, yarn over, insert hook into next stitch, yarn over, draw through the work, yarn over, draw through 2 loops, yarn over, draw through all 3 loops, leaving just 1 loop.

finishing off

The finish is an important part of making a project, so don't be tempted to rush the final stages. Time and care are essential for a neat and tidy finish, especially when joining pieces.

Fastening off

Cut the yarn, leaving roughly 5 in (13 cm). (If you are going to be sewing up a seam, you should leave a longer tail). Make 1 chain and draw the tail through the chain and pull firmly. Weave the end an inch or a few centimeters in one direction and then back the other way for a neat and secure finish.

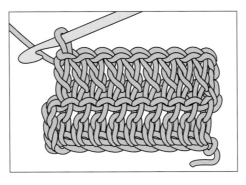

Pressing

Where the pattern requires you to press your work, place the item under a piece of damp cloth and iron flat. Metallic yarn or thread items will benefit especially from pressing, but fluffy yarns and textured stitches, such as loop stitches, should be left alone so as not to spoil the look of the fabric.

Seams

There are various ways of sewing up seams. Two principal methods are given here: joining the seams edge to edge using flat stitch and slip-stitch seams. Flat stitch creates an almost invisible, ridgeless seam. Slip stitch is stronger and most suited to seams where minimal stretch is required.

To fasten off, make 1 chain, draw the tail through the chain, and pull firmly.

tips & hints

- For all sewing, use a blunt-tipped tapestry needle that won't split yarn.

Slip stitch

This seam uses a crochet hook and creates a very firm join, suitable for bags or other items that do not need much flexibility. With right sides together, insert the hook into the first stitch of both sections, yarn over the hook, and draw the loop through both stitches and the loop on the hook. Repeat along the length of the seam.

Flat stitch

This seam is sewn with a tapestry needle and creates an almost invisible join. It is used when the number of stitches is the same on both pieces. Lay the 2 sections right side up with the stitches aligned. Insert the needle under the lower half of the edge stitch on one section, then under the upper half of the edge stitch on the opposite section. Repeat along the length of the seam.

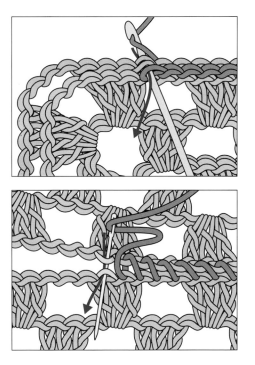

flowers and motifs

Crochet is a great way to customize your clothes. Adding decorative motifs is a fun way of revamping an old garment, adding to a new one, or simply making a change.

Learn how to make flowers, fruit, and other simple motifs that can be sewn or even just pinned onto existing clothes or shoes. Most of the ideas in this section require only very small quantities of yarn, so it's a great way to use up any odds and ends you may have left over from other projects.

Once you've mastered a few of the basic techniques shown here, the possibilities are limitless!

Motifs are generally symmetrical designs that can be used individually (as we are doing here) or used in multiples and sewn together to create patchworks and other items. Because they're so quick to make and use very little yarn, they are a great way to customize your clothes easily and inexpensively.

Here are 4 simple motifs that can be sewn directly onto your clothes or used with a pin to make a brooch.

Daisy

This is a simple and versatile daisy motif with petals made of chain stitches.

Materials
Cotton Glace from Rowan in Hyacinth
E (3.5 mm) crochet hook

Ch 6 and join in a ring with a sl st.
Round 1: Work 14 sc into ring, sl st to first sc at beg of round to close.
Round 2: Work (1 sc, ch 6, 1 sc) into fl only of each sc. Sl st to first sc to close.
Round 3: Work (1 sc, ch 8, 1 sc) into bl only of each sc, sl st to first sc to close.

Fasten off.
You can either attach a brooch pin to the back or simply use a safety pin.

Rose

Here is an easy three-dimensional rose that can be worn on a hat, bag, jacket, jeans—anywhere!

Materials
Cotton Glace from Rowan in Candy Floss
E (3.5 mm) crochet hook
Ch 8 and join into a ring with a sl st.

Round 1: Ch 6 (count as 1 dc and 3 ch), *1 dc into ring, ch 3; rep from * 4 more times, sl st into 3rd ch of beg ch 6.
Round 2: Work 1 petal (1 sc, 1 hdc, 3 dc, 1 hdc, 1 sc) into each ch-3 sp.
Round 3: *Ch 5, 1 sc into last sc of next petal; rep from * ending with ch 5.
Round 4: Work 1 petal (1 sc, 1 hdc, 5 dc, 1 hdc, 1 sc) into each ch-5 sp.
Round 5: *Ch 7, 1 sc into last sc of next petal; rep from * ending with ch 7.
Round 6: Work 1 petal (1 sc, 1 hdc, 7 dc, 1 hdc, 1 sc) into each ch-7 sp, sl st to first sc.
Fasten off.

Photo at left: A contrasting daisy stitched to a bikini bottom

Photo on opposite page: A rose worn as a brooch

Cherries

A simple and bold design, these three-dimensional cherries look almost good enough to eat! They would look fantastic sewn onto a hat or jacket, or suspended from a brooch.

Materials
Cotton Glace from Rowan in Poppy and Shoot
E (3.5 mm) crochet hook

Special abbreviation
tr: triple crochet—yo twice, insert hook into work, yo, draw through work, yo, draw through first 2 loops, yo, draw through next 2 loops, yo, draw through last 2 loops.

Fruit—make 2
Ch 4.

Row 1: 8 tr into 4th ch from hook, turn.

Row 2: Ch 3, *leaving last loop of each tr on hook, work 1 tr into each of next 4 tr, yo, draw through all 5 loops on hook; rep from * once more. Fasten off.

Leaves
First leaf
Ch 10.

Round 1: 1 sc into 2nd ch from hook, 1 hdc into next ch, 1 dc into each of next 3 ch, work 1 tr into next ch, 1 dc into next ch, 1 hdc into next

ch, 1 sc into last ch. Do not turn.

Round 2: Ch 1, 1 sc into bottom loop of each ch, work (1 sc, ch 1, 1 sc) into first ch of rnd 1, 1 sc into each st to end.

Sl st into starting ch. Do not fasten off.

Second leaf
Ch 10.

Round 1: 1 sc into 2nd ch from hook, 1 hdc into next ch, 1 dc into each of next 3 ch, work 1 tr into next ch, 1 dc into next ch, 1 hdc into next ch, 1 sc into last ch. Turn.

Round 2: Ch 1, 1 sc into each st, work (1 sc, ch 1, 1 sc) into first ch, 1 sc into bottom loop of each ch to next to last ch, sl st into last ch. Fasten off.

Use brown or black yarn of a similar weight to attach the cherries to the leaves with a series of chains.

Star

This star is easy to make. It can be worn individually or it can be made into an interesting patchwork fabric by making lots of identical stars and sewing them together.

Materials
Cotton Glace from Rowan in Zeal
E (3.5 mm) crochet hook

Special abbreviation
tr: triple crochet—yo twice, insert hook into work, yo, draw through work, yo, draw through first 2 loops, yo, draw through last 2 loops.

Ch 2.

Round 1: 5 sc into 2nd ch from hook.

Round 2: 3 sc into each sc.

Round 3: *1 sc into next st, ch 6, sl st in 2nd ch from hook, 1 sc into next ch, 1 hdc into next ch, 1 dc into next ch, 1 tr into next ch, 1 tr into base of starting sc, skip 2 sc; rep from * 4 more times. Sl st into first sc to join.

Round 4: *Working into the bottom loop of each ch on round 3, work 1 sc into each ch, (1 sc, ch 1, 1 sc) into tch, 1 sc into each of next 6 sts, sl st into next sc; rep from * 4 more times.
Fasten off.

edgings and inserts

Crochet is the ideal way to add edgings to the cuffs or hem of an old cardigan or a plain sweater that needs enlivening. Here are 5 funky edgings to add pizzazz to your clothes!

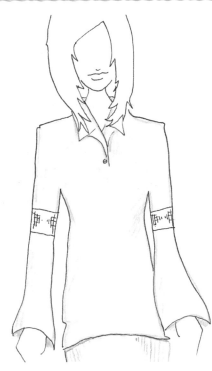

If you are crocheting directly onto your clothes, use a yarn that is of a similar weight to the garment you are customizing. If the weight of the yarn and size of the stitches differs greatly, work 1 row of single crochet of an intermediate weight yarn around the edge to create an even base for your decorative trim. To add edgings to woven fabrics, make the trimming first and sew it on afterward.

> **tips & hints**
> - For a neat look, start at the garment seam.

Crab stitch border

This is a very simple border using single crochet worked from left to right, instead of right to left as normal. It can be worked on any number of stitches and is a good way of finishing off a crocheted item, especially if you use a contrasting color.

Join yarn at the seam. Working from left to right, insert hook into next stitch, yarn over, draw through the work, yarn over, and draw through both loops. Fasten off.

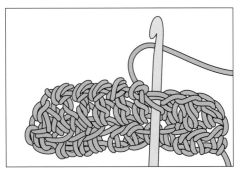

Above left: Crochet insert in the sleeves of a cotton tunic.

Shell border

This is a very simple but effective border, which creates a pretty shell effect on a knitted or crocheted garment, especially on a cuff or hem.

Join the yarn at a seam, and work 1 round of single crochet evenly around the edge of the fabric.
Make sure the final number of stitches is a multiple of 6. (To work a separate trim, work a base chain adding 2 chains for a multiple of 6 plus 2. Work 1 row of single crochet.)
Join with a sl st to first sc.
*Skip 2 sts, 5 dc into next st, skip 2 sts, 1 sl st into next st; rep from * to end, sl st into sl st at beg.
Fasten off.

Right: The shell border has an attractive scalloped edge.
Far right: Picot border

Picot border

This is a very pretty edging for a demure look!

Join the yarn at a seam, and work 1 round of single crochet evenly around the edge of the fabric. Make sure the final number of stitches is a multiple of 3. (To work a separate trim, work a base chain adding 2 chains for a multiple of 3 plus 2. Work 1 row of single crochet.) Join with a sl st to first sc.
*1 sl st into each of next 2 sts, 1 sc into next st, ch 3, 1 sc in same st as last sc; rep from * to end, sl st into first st. Fasten off.

Arches border

This is a fun, lacy border with 2 rows of arches. It is great for adding a bit of length to a cuff or hem.

Join the yarn at a seam and work 1 round of single crochet evenly around the edge of the fabric. Make sure the final number of stitches is a multiple of 7 plus 1. (To work a separate trim, work a base chain adding 3 chains for a multiple of 7 plus 3. Work 1 row of single crochet).
Join with a sl st to first sc.

Round 1: Ch 3 (count as 1 dc), skip 1 sc, 1 dc into each sc to end, sl st into top of ch of beg ch 3.

Round 2: Ch 1, 1 sc into each of first 2 dc, * ch 7, skip 4 dc, 1 sc into each of next 3 dc; rep from * to end, omitting 1 sc at end of last rep, sl st into first sc.

Round 3: Ch 1, 1 sc into each of first 2 sc, *7 sc into ch-7 sp, 1 sc into each of next 3 sc; rep from * to end omitting 1 sc at end of last rep, sl st into first sc.

Round 4: Ch 7 (count as 1 hdc, ch 3), skip 4 sc, 1 sc into each of next 3 sc, * ch 7, skip 7 sc, 1 sc into each of next 3 sc; rep from * to last 4 sc, ch 3, 1 hdc into last sc, sl st to 4th ch of beg ch 7.

Round 5: Ch 1, 3 sc into ch-3 sp, *1 sc into each of next 3 sc, 7 sc into ch-7 sp, rep from * to end, working 3 sc into last ch-3 sp, sl st into first sc.
Fasten off.

Frills and spills

Here's a really quick and easy way to make an unusual trim using fronds of chains worked first into the front and then into the back of a row of single crochet.

Join the yarn at a seam, and work 1 round of single crochet evenly around the edge of the fabric. Any number of stitches will work with this trim.
Join with a sl st into first sc.

Round 1: *Ch 7, sl st into the fl only of the next st; rep from * to end.

Round 2: *Ch 7, sl st into the bl only of the next st; rep from * to end, sl st into first st.
Fasten off.

Left: Arches border

Right: Frills and spills border

Filet insert

Filet is an ancient and traditional method of making decorative edgings. This section explains how, using a fine yarn, you can make pretty and interesting bands of filet crochet to insert into a sleeve or bodice.

The principle of filet crochet is that it is made from a network of double and chain stitches. You can make interesting patterns using open squares and blocks (represented by dots on the chart below). Use a sheet of graph paper to plot your pattern: in each blank square a double is skipped and a chain worked; in each blocked square a double is worked into every stitch.

You can either follow the pattern shown here or make your own design. Simple symmetrical designs will work best. And unless you are using a very fine yarn the band should be no more than 10 squares wide. When calculating the length of the base chain, work on number of squares x 2 + 3 (count as first double).

To make the insert shown here:
Ch 21, 1 dc into 5th ch from hook, *ch 1, skip 1 ch, 1 st into next ch; rep from * to end. For each empty square work 1 ch, skip 1 dc, 1 dc into next st. For each filled square, work 1 dc into each st, (including ch). Work last dc into 3rd ch of beg ch 4.

Follow the pattern until the band is the correct length for the garment into which you wish to insert it. Fasten off.

Edging
To give the insert a pretty finish, work a picot border along each of the long edges as follows:
Work (1 sc, ch 1, 1 sc) into each row end.

Finishing
To attach your insert, sew one side by hand or machine to the edge of your garment. Then with the wrong side facing, sew up your band seam. Finally, sew the opposite edge of the insert to the corresponding edge of your garment.

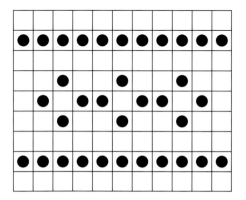

Left: A filet insert band, with an example of a filet chart.

collars and cuffs

Surface crochet is the method of adding texture to knitted or crocheted fabric. It can be used to add interest to cuffs and collars as we've done here, or to apply motifs and patterns to a knitted or crocheted garment for a radical new look.

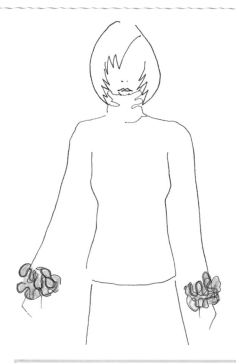

Bahamas Palm Fronds

Add a tropical touch to your clothes with this spike stitch border.

Materials
Cotton Glace from Rowan in Shoot
E (3.5 mm) crochet hook

Round 1: Ch 1, work a round of sc evenly around edge, ensuring the final number of sts is a multiple of 4, sl st into first ch.
Round 2: Ch 1, 1 sc into each of first 2 sts, *insert hook into fabric to the right of the next st, pick up yarn and draw up to height of edge, work directly below and to the left in the same way, insert hook into next st, yo, draw loop through, yo, draw through all 5 loops, 1 sc into each of next 3 sts; rep from * to end, sl st into first ch. Fasten off. Weave in all ends.

Opposite: Here are some of the great cuffs you can crochet—some of which would also work well as an edging around the neckline, too! Clockwise, from bottom left: Bahamas Palm Fronds; Amazing Yarn—frilly edge; Raised Wave Cuff; and Midas Ribs.

Amazing Yarn—frilly edge

With the really interesting yarns available, you can make radical changes with simple techniques.

Materials
Fizz from Sirdar in Carnival
E (3.5 mm) crochet hook

Round 1: Ch 1, work a round of sc evenly around edge so that you are left with an odd number of sts, sl st into first ch to join.
Round 2: *Ch 6, skip next sc, 1 sc into next sc; rep from * to end.
Round 3: Ch 3, *1 sc into ch-6 space, ch 6; rep from * to end, working last sc into beg ch-3 space. Fasten off.

Raised Wave Cuff

This trim is worked in 2 tiers to stand out from the cuff. This works with a multiple of 7 single crochets.

Materials
Cotton Glace from Rowan in Poppy
E (3.5 mm) crochet hook

Round 1: Ch 1, work a round of sc evenly around edge ensuring the final number of sts is a multiple of 7, sl st to first sc.
Round 2: Work 1 st into each sc as follows: *1 sc, 1

hdc, 1 dc, 1 tr, 1 dc, 1 hdc, 1 sc; rep from * to end.

Round 3: Work 1 st into each st of round 2: *1 sc, 1 hdc, 1 dc, 1 tr, 1 dc, 1 hdc, 1 sc; rep from * to end.

Round 4: Work 1 st into the base of each st of round 2: *1 sc, 1 hdc, 1 dc, 1 tr, 1 dc, 1 hdc, 1 sc; rep from * to end.

Round 5: Work 1 st into each st of round 4: *1 sc, 1 hdc, 1 dc, 1 tr, 1 dc, 1 hdc, 1 sc; rep from * to end.
Fasten off.

Open out the 2 tiers and press flat.

Midas Ribs

Metallic fingering yarn worked onto the surface of cuffs in ribs of uneven length creates a glamorous gilded edge. Working single crochet into the surface of the fabric is no different than regular single crochet: insert the hook into the fabric from front to back and then from back to front so the hook emerges a short distance from where it went in (this will be the length of the stitch), yarn over, draw loop through fabric, yarn over, and draw through remaining 2 loops.

Materials
2 mm crochet hook
Metallic fingering yarn in gold

Round 1: Ch 1, work sc around the cuff edge so that the final number of sts is a multiple of 4, sl st to first sc.

Round 2: Ch 1, 1 sc into first sc, *work a row of sc

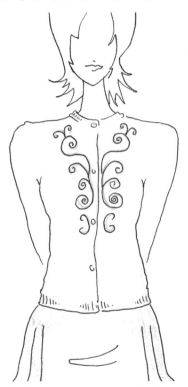

into the fabric perpendicular to cuff edge, approximately 8 sts, turn, skip first sc, 1 sc into each sc until you reach cuff edge, 1 sc into each of next 3 sc along cuff edge; rep from * working a different number of sts for each rib, sl st into first sc.

Round 3: Ch 1, 1 sc into each sc around cuff edge, sl st into first sc. Fasten off.

Weave in all ends.

Crochet collars

There are many possibilities with crochet. Use any of the edgings or cuff suggestions to liven up a dull neckline, or for a purely decorative effect, use surface crochet to create any pattern you like. To achieve the best results, when crocheting onto a premade knitted or crocheted garment, select a yarn that is similar in weight to that used in the fabric. If the knit is very fine, as is shown here, you should also use a fine yarn and a small hook; otherwise, you will not be able to draw the hook and the yarn through the fabric.

Materials
2 mm crochet hook
Kid Silk Haze from Rowan in Marmalade

First, decide on your design. If it is complicated or requires symmetry, use a dressmaker's pencil to mark your design directly onto the fabric.

Thread the yarn through from the wrong side of the work to the front (or right side) of the garment so that the tail is on the wrong side and the ball at the front(or right side) of the garment. Insert hook into and back out of the fabric and draw through a loop, yarn over, and draw through 2 loops. Continue to work in this way, following the pencil markings (or you could go freestyle and work where your hook takes you!). If you are using a very fine yarn, you might want to work 2 or 3 rows so that your design really stands out.

patches and pockets

Here are 4 funky pockets or patches that can be stitched anywhere and onto anything!
Add interest and color to your jeans, brighten up a dull bag, or even join several patches
to make a cushion or a small throw.

Two of these designs use color, the first in a traditional square motif known as a granny square. Individually these can be used to make pockets (or items such as placemats), but sewn together in multiples, they can also be used to make much larger items like a patchwork throw or, as is shown later on in the book, to make a granny squares scarf. The second design uses 2 colors to make zigzag stripes.

The other 2 pockets use textured stitches: one a busy bobbly pocket and the other an ingenious way of making crochet fur. All the pockets can be made in any size with any yarn. The materials used here are just a guideline—let your imagination run free!

Above: A traditional square motif, known as a granny square

Multicolored granny square

For a bright pocket or patch for your jeans, this is a fun and bold design using 6 colors. It's a great way to use up odds and ends of yarn. Remember, the thicker the yarn, the bigger the patch!

Special abbreviation

tr: triple crochet—yo twice, insert hook into work, yo, draw through work, yo, draw through first 2 loops, yo, draw through next 2 loops, yo, draw through last 2 loops.

Materials

A small quantity of Cotton Glace from Rowan in
   6 different colors
E (3.5 mm) crochet hook

Using color A, ch 4, join into a ring with a sl st into first ch.

Round 1: Ch 4, 3 tr into ring (ch 2, 4 tr into ring) 3 times, ch 2, sl st to 4th ch of beg ch 4. Break off A and turn.

Round 2: Join color B to next ch-2 sp, 2 sc into same space * 1 sc into each of next 4 sts, [2 sc, ch 2, 2 sc] into corner ch-2 space; rep from * twice more, 1 sc into each of next 4 sts, 2 sc into same ch sp as join, ch 2, sl st to first sc. Break off B and turn.

Round 3: Join color C to first sc after a ch-2 sp, ch 3, 1 dc into ch-2 sp before join, *(skip next sc, 1 dc into next sc, 1 dc into skipped sc) 3 times, skip 1 sc, 1 dc into next ch-2 sp, 1 dc into skipped sc, 1 dc into next sc, 1 dc into ch-2 sp; rep from * twice more, (skip next sc, 1 dc into next sc, 1 dc into skipped sc) 3 times, skip 1 sc, 1 dc into ch-2 sp, 1 dc into skipped sc, join with a sl st to 3rd ch of beg ch 3. Break off C and turn.

Round 4: Join color D to same place as join of last round, ch 3, 2 dc into same place as join (ch 1, 3 dc into next dc, 1 dc into next 8 dc, 3 dc into next dc) 4 times omitting 3 dc at end of last rep, sl st to 3rd ch of beg ch 3. Break off D and turn.

Round 5: Join color E to first dc after next ch-1 sp. 1 sc into same place as join, 1 sc into next dc, *(1 tr into next dc, then bending tr in half to form bobble on RS of square, work 1 sc into next dc, 1 sc into next dc) 4 times, 3 dc into corner ch-1 sp, 1 sc into each of next 2 dc, rep from * 3 times omitting 2 sc at end of last rep, sl st to first sc. Break off E and turn.

Round 6: Join color F to first sc of any side, ch 3 (1 dc into each st to center dc of 3 dc at corner, 3 dc into corner dc) 4 times, 1 dc in next dc, sl st to 3rd ch of beg ch 3. Fasten off.

Finishing

Gently press patch flat. Weave in all ends. Either sew all 4 sides to your garment, or sew up just 3 sides, leaving the top open to make a pocket.

Bobble pocket

Dare to be different with this textured, bobbly pocket. It's quick and fun to make, and ideal for spicing up a plain cardigan or sweater.

Materials

1 x 1.75 oz (50 g) ball of Snuggly DK from Sirdar in Flamenco
H (5 mm) crochet hook

Above: A textured, bobble pocket is really easy.

Special abbreviations

Make a bobble by working dc5tog as follows: *yo, insert hook into st, yo, draw through work, yo, draw through 2 loops; rep from * 4 times, yo, draw through all 6 loops.

Ch 27 (or any multiple of 4 + 3).

Row 1: Skip 3 ch (count as 1 dc in this and following rows), 1 dc into each ch to end, turn.

Row 2: Ch 1, 1 sc into each of first 2 sts, *work dc5tog into next st, 1 sc into each of next 3 sts; rep from * to last 3 sts, work dc5tog into next st, 1 sc into each of last 2 sts, including top of beg ch 1, turn.

Row 3: Ch 3, skip first st, 1 dc into each st to end, turn.

Row 4: Ch 1, 1 sc into each of first 4 sts, *work dc5tog into next st, 1 sc into each of next 3 sts; rep from * 1 sc into top of beg ch 1, turn.

Row 5: Ch 3, skip first st, 1 dc into each st to end, turn.

Rep rows 2–5 until you have a square. Do not fasten off.

Edging

Work 1 round of sc evenly around the edge of your pocket, working 3 sc at each corner. Join with a sl st to first sc. Fasten off.

Zigzag pocket

As the pattern is quite large, it is best to use a fairly fine yarn to make the most of this two-tone zigzag pattern.

Materials

1 x 1.75 oz (50 g) ball of Cotton Glace from Rowan in Shoot (color A) and Excite (color B)
E (3.5 mm) crochet hook

Using color A, ch 35 (or any multiple of 11 + 2).

Row 1: 2 sc into 2nd ch from hook, *1 sc into each of next 4 ch, skip 2 ch, 1 sc into each of next 4 ch, 3 sc into next ch; rep from * working only 2 sc into last ch, turn.

Above: A cool, geometric zigzag!

Row 2: Ch 1, 2 sc into first st, *1 sc into each of next 4 sts, skip 2 sts, 1 sc into each of next 4 sts, 3 sc into next st; rep from * working only 2 sc into last st, turn.
Rep row 2 twice more.
Change to color B. Work row 2 four times. Alternating between the 2 colors, work 5 bands of color.

Edging

Using color B, ch 1, work 1 sc into each row end along the side of the pocket, then work 1 sc into first ch of base ch, 1 hdc into next ch, 1 dc into each of next 2 ch, 1 tr into next ch. Work 2 sc into the side of the tr you've just made, 1 sc into the base of the tr. Work 1 st into each st of base ch as follows: *1 sc into first of 2 ch at point, skip 2nd of these ch, 1 sc into next ch, 1 hdc into next ch, 1 dc into each of next 2 ch, 1 tr into next ch, 1 dc into each of next 2 ch, 1 hdc into next ch, 1 sc into next ch; rep from * ending 1 tr. Work 2 sc into the side of the tr and 1 sc into the base of the tr, 1 sc into each row end to top of pocket. Fasten off.

Finishing

Press pocket gently and sew, crochet, or glue to your clothes using fabric glue.

Magic garden pocket

Make an amazing realistic grass pocket using loop stitches. Cutting the loops makes it look like blades of grass! Add a flower to complete your own miniature crochet garden!

Materials

1 x 1 oz (25 g) ball of Bonus Toytime from Sirdar in Apple
1 x 1 oz (25 g) ball of Bonus Toytime from Sirdar in Popsicle
H (5 mm) crochet hook

Special abbreviation

loop st: This is a very simple variation on sc. Hold the work and yarn as if to sc. Insert hook into work as if to sc, pick up the yarn on both sides of the loop made by your finger (see illustration on page 62), and draw the 2 strands through the stitch, yo and draw all loops through on hook.

Pocket

Using Apple, ch 21 (or any number of sts).
Row 1: 1 sc into 2nd ch from hook and each ch to end, turn.
Row 2: Ch 1, 1 loop st into each st to end, turn.
Row 3: Ch 1, 1 sc into each st to end.
Rep rows 2 and 3 until pocket is 5 in (13 cm) high ending on a row 3.
Fasten off.

Now for the fun part. Take a pair of scissors and cut each of the loops at the center top of the loop to make the fabric look like grass.

Flower

Using Popsicle, ch 6 and join in a ring with sl st.
Round 1: 14 sc into ring, sl st to first sc at beg of round to close.
Round 2: Work (1 sc, ch 6, 1 sc) into fl only of each sc, sl st to first sc to close.
Round 3: Work (1 sc, ch 8, 1 sc) into bl only of each sc, sl st to first sc to close.
Fasten off.

Sew flower onto grassy pocket.

project index

Here's a gallery of all the specially designed projects featured in the book. They use a range of interesting new yarns to help create a truly unique look. Once you have become familiar with the basic techniques, you'll find all these projects easy and fun to make.

Beret   40

Froth and frills scarf   53

Granny squares scarf   54

Beads and tassels scarf   56

Basic round bag   58

Swirl bag   68

Gold sparkly belt   70

Flower hipster belt   73

Wrist cuff and choker   74

Frilly mini   84

Fluffy shawl   87

Peep shoulder poncho   88

Sparkly halterneck   90

project index

beret

Get the Parisian chic look with this classic round beret, perfect all year round. It is crocheted in a spiral using just single crochet. The variegated wool gives it a fantastic textured look.

Materials
2 x 3.5 oz (100 g) skeins of Point Five from Colinette in Neptune
M (9 mm) crochet hook

Size
Small to medium; large
Beginning with round 9, instructions for smaller size are given first, larger size following smaller size.

Skill
Easy

Gauge
8 sts and 9 rows to 4 in (10 cm) measured over rows of sc using M (9 mm hook)

Special abbreviations
sc2tog: insert hook into next st, yo, draw through the work, insert hook into next st, yo, draw through the work, yo and draw through all 3 loops, leaving just 1 loop.

Pattern
Ch 4, and join into a ring with a sl st.
Round 1: Ch 1, work 7 sc into the ring.
Round 2: 2 sc into each sc to end—14 sts.
Round 3: *1 sc into next st, 2 sc into next st; rep from * to end—21 sts.
Round 4: *1 sc into each of next 2 sts, 2 sc into next st; rep from * to end—28 sts.

Round 5: *1 sc into each of next 3 sts, 2 sc into next st; rep from * to end—35 sts.
Round 6: *1 sc into each of next 4 sts, 2 sc into next st; rep from * to end—42 sts.
Round 7: 1 sc into each sc to end.
Round 8: *1 sc into each of next 5 sts, 2 sc into next st; rep from * to end—49 sts.

Small/medium beret
Rounds 9, 10, and 11: 1 sc into each sc to end.
Round 12: *1 sc into each of next 5 sc, sc2tog; rep from * to end—42 sts.
Round 13: *1 sc into each of next 4 sc, sc2tog; rep from * to end—35 sts.
Round 14: *1 sc into each of next 3 sc, sc2tog; rep from * to end—28 sts.
Round 15: 1 sc into each sc. At the end of the round, join to first sc of previous round with a sl st. Fasten off and weave in yarn end.

Large beret
Round 9: 1 sc into each sc to end.
Round 10: 1 sc in each of next 8 sc, 2 sc in next sc; rep from * to last 4 sc, 1 sc in each of last 4 sc—54 sts.
Round 11: 1 sc into each sc to end.
Round 12: *1 sc into each of next 4 sc, sc2tog; rep from * to end—45 sts.
Round 13: *1 sc into each of next 3 sc, sc2tog; rep from * to end—36 sts.
Round 14: 1 sc into each sc to end.

Round 15: 1 sc into each sc to end. At the end of the round, join to first sc of previous round with a sl st. Fasten off and sew in yarn end.

---

tips & hints
- If you need to tighten the beret to fit, thread shirring elastic around the edge

cloche hat

This pretty cloche hat with its shell border is inspired by the 1920s. You could also add a decorative flower pin to it. The cool cotton yarn makes it perfect for spring or summer.

Materials
2 x 1.25 oz (50g) ball of All Seasons Cotton from Rowan in Soul
1 x 1.75 oz (50 g) ball of All Seasons Cotton from Rowan in Jaunty
7 (4.5 mm) crochet hook

Size
Small, medium, large

Skill
Easy

Gauge
14 sts and 17 rows to 4 in (10 cm) measured over rows of sc using 7 (4.5 mm) hook

Pattern
Ch 4, join into a ring with a sl st.
Round 1: 8 sc into ring.
Round 2: 2 sc into each sc—16 sts.
Round 3: *1 sc into next sc, 2 sc into next sc; rep from * to end—24 sts.
Round 4: *1 sc into each of next 2 sc, 2 sc into next sc; rep from * to end—32 sts.
Round 5: *1 sc into each of next 3 sc, 2 sc into next sc; rep from * to end—40 sts.
Round 6: *1 sc into each of next 4 sc, 2 sc into next sc; rep from * to end—48 sts.

Round 7: *1 sc into each of next 5 sc, 2 sc into next sc; rep from * to end—56 sts.
Round 8: *1 sc into each of next 6 sc, 2 sc into next sc; rep from * to end—64 sts.
Round 9: 1 sc into each sc to end.
Round 10: *1 sc into each of next 7 sc, 2 sc into next sc; rep from * to end—72 sts.
Round 11: 1 sc into each sc to end.

Medium and large size
Round 12: *1 sc into each of next 8 sc, 2 sc into next sc; rep from * to end—80 sts.
Round 13: 1 sc in each sc to end.

Large size only
Round 14: *1 sc into each of next 9 sc, 2 sc into next sc; rep from * to end—88 sts.

All sizes
Cont to work straight until hat measures 6 3/4 in (17 cm) from crown.

Brim (instructions for larger sizes in parentheses)
Next round: *1 sc into each of next 8 (9, 10) sc, 2 sc into next sc; rep from * to end—80 (88, 96) sts.
Next round: *1 sc into each of next 9 (10, 11) sc, 2 sc into next sc; rep from * to end—88 (96, 104) sts.

Next round: *1 sc into each of next 10 (11, 12) sc, 2 sc into next sc; rep from * to end—96 (104, 112) sts.
Next round: *1 sc into each of next 11 (12, 13) sc, 2 sc into next sc; rep from * to end, sl st to first sc—104 (112, 120) sts.
Next round: shell edging
*Skip 1 sc, 5 dc into next sc, skip 1 sc, 1 sc into next sc; rep from * to end, sl st into sl st of previous rnd.
Fasten off.

Flower pin
Ch 6 and join in a ring with sl st.
Round 1: 14 sc into ring, sl st to sc at beg of rnd to close.
Round 2: Work 1 petal (1 sc, ch 6, 1 sc) into fl only of each sc, sl st to first sc to close.
Round 3: Work 1 petal (1 sc, ch 8, 1 sc) into bl of each sc, sl st to first sc to close.
Fasten off.

You can either attach a brooch pin to the back of the flower or simply use a safety pin to attach it to the hat.

russian hat

Here is a new-look beret modeled after the Russian onion domes. This unusual shape is created by varying the rate of increase as the hat grows from crown to brim. Bobbles have been incorporated into the fabric to add interest and a gold trim worked around the bottom.

Materials
2 x 3.5 oz (100 g) balls of Denim Chunky from Sirdar in Ivory Cream
7 (4.5 mm) crochet hook
D (3.25 mm) crochet hook
Small quantity of metallic fingering yarn in gold

Size
Small to medium; large

Skill
Easy

Gauge
15 sts and 16 rows to 4 in (10 cm) measured over rows of sc using 7 (4.5 mm) hook

Special abbreviations
sc2tog: insert hook into next st, yo, draw through the work, insert hook into next st, yo and draw through the work, yo and draw through all 3 loops, leaving just 1 loop.

Bobble: make a bobble by working a number of sts into the same st, and joining them at the top. In this pattern the bobble is made of 4 dc: leaving last loop of each dc on hook work 4 dc in same st, yo, draw through all 5 loops.

Pattern
Ch 4, join in a ring with a sl st.
Round 1: 4 sc into ring.
Round 2: 2 sc into each sc to end—8 sts.
Round 3: *1 sc into next sc, 2 sc into next sc; rep from * to end—12 sts.
Round 4: *1 sc into each of next 2 sc, 2 sc into next sc; rep from * to end—16 sts.
Round 5: *1 sc into each of next 3 sc, 2 sc into next sc; rep from * to end—20 sts.
Round 6: *1 sc into each of next 4 sc, 2 sc into next sc; rep from * to end—24 sts.
Round 7: *1 sc into each of next 5 sc, 2 sc into next sc; rep from * to end—28 sts.
Round 8: *1 sc into each of next 6 sc, 2 sc into next sc; rep from * to end—32 sts.
Round 9: *1 sc into each of next 7 sc, 2 sc into next sc; rep from * to end—36 sts.
Round 10: *1 sc into each of next 8 sc, 2 dc into next sc; rep from * to end—40 sts.
Round 11: *1 sc into each of next 9 sc, 2 sc into next sc; rep from * to end—44 sts.
Round 12: *1 sc into each of next 10 sc, 2 sc into next sc; rep from * to end—48 sts.
Round 13: *1 sc into each of next 11 sc, 2 sc into next sc; rep from * to end—52 sts.
Round 14: *1 sc into each of next 12 sc, 2 sc into next sc; rep from * to end—56 sts.

Bobbles
Work 1 bobble per round from rows 15 to 29. You should space these so that they appear evenly arranged when the hat is finished.
Round 15: *1 sc into each of next 6 sc, 2 sc into next sc; rep from * to end—64 sts.
Round 16: *1 sc into each of next 7 sc, 2 sc into next sc; rep from * to end—72 sts.
Round 17: *1 sc into each of next 8 sc, 2 sc into next sc; rep from * to end—80 sts.
Round 18: *1 sc into each of next 9 sc, 2 dc into next sc; rep from * to end—88 sts.
Round 19: *1 sc into each of next 10 sc, 2 sc into next sc; rep from * to end—96 sts.
Round 20: *1 sc into each of next 11 sc, 2 sc into next sc; rep from * to end—104 sts.

Small–medium
Rounds 21–25: Work straight without increasing.
Round 26: *1 sc into each of next 11 sc, sc2tog; rep from * to end—96 sts.
Round 27: *1 sc into each of next 10 sc, sc2tog; rep from * to end—88 sts.
Round 28: *1 sc into each of next 9 sc, sc2tog; rep from * to end—80 sts.
Round 29: *1 sc into each of next 8 sc, sc2tog; rep from * to end—72 sts.
Rounds 30–38: Work straight without decreasing. Join with a sl st to first sc.
Fasten off.

Large

Round 21: *1 sc into each of next 24 sc, 2 sc into next sc; rep from * to end—108 sts.

Rounds 22–26: Work straight without increasing.

Round 27: *1 sc into each of next 25 sc, sc2tog; rep from * to end—104 sts.

Round 28: *1 sc into each of next 11 sc, sc2tog; rep from * to end—96 sts.

Round 29: *1 sc into each of next 10 sc, sc2tog; rep from * to end—88 sts.

Round 30: *1 sc into each of next 9 sc, sc2tog; rep from * to end—80 sts.

Rounds 31–39: Work straight without decreasing. Join with a sl st to first sc.

Fasten off.

Edging

With right side facing and D (3.25 mm) hook, attach gold yarn to brim, work 1 sc into each sc to end. Join with a sl st to first sc.

Fasten off.

Finishing

Weave in all ends.

stripy mittens

These super-chunky, stripy mittens are easy to make, with a ribbed cuff and alternating colors worked in single crochet. They will keep hands warm on the chilliest of days.

Materials
1 x 3.5 oz (100 g) ball of Bonus Chunky from Sirdar in Denim (color A)
1 x 3.5 oz (100 g) ball of Bonus Chunky from Sirdar in Bluebell (color B)
I (5.5 mm) crochet hook
K (6.5 mm) crochet hook
Shirring elastic

Size
Measured from wrist bone to middle finger tip:
Small: 6½–7 in (16.5–18 cm)
Medium: 7–7½ in (18–19 cm)
Large: 7½–8 in (19–20.5 cm)
Instructions for small size are given first. Larger sizes are in parentheses.

Skill
Easy

Gauge
11 sts and 12 rows to 4 in (10 cm) measured over rows of sc using K (6.5 mm) hook

Special abbreviations
sc BLO—sc into the back loop only.

sc2tog: insert hook into next st, yo, draw through the work, insert hook into next st, yo and draw through the work, yo and draw through all 3 loops, leaving just 1 loop.

Pattern
Right mitten
Cuff
Using color A and I (5.5 mm) hook, ch 9.
Row 1: 1 sc into 2nd ch from hook, 1 ch into each sc to end (8 sts). Turn.
Row 2: Ch 1, sc BLO into each st to end.
Rep this row 21 (23, 25) more times.
Do not fasten off.

Join cuff by working sl sts into corresponding sts of last row and bottom loop of base ch. Turn cuff inside out. This is now the right side.
Change to K (6.5 mm) hook and attach color B.
Round 1: Ch 1, 1 sc into end of each row. Join to beg ch 1 with a sl st—23 (25, 27) sts.
Round 2: Ch 1, 1 sc into each st to end. Join to beg ch 1 with a sl st.
Rounds 3–5: Rep round 2 three more times.
Round 6: Using color A, ch 1, 1 sc into first st, ch 5 to make thumbhole, skip 4 sc, 1 sc into each sc to end. Join to beg ch 1 with a sl st.
Round 7: Ch 1, 1 sc into first st, 1 sc into each ch, 1 sc into each st to end. Join to beg ch 1 with a sl st—24 (26, 28) sts.
Rounds 8–10: Ch 1, 1 sc into each st to end. Join to beg ch 1 with a sl st.
Round 11: Using color B, ch 1, sc2tog, 1 sc into each of next 10 (11, 12) sts, sc2tog, 1 sc into each st to end. Join to beg ch 1 with a sl st—22 (24, 26) sts.

Round 12: Ch 1, 1 sc into each st to end. Join to beg ch 1 with a sl st.
Round 13: Ch 1, sc2tog, 1 sc into each of next 9 (10, 11) sts, sc2tog, 1 sc into each st to end. Join to beg ch 1 with a sl st—20 (22, 24) sts.
Round 14: 1 ch, 1 sc into each st to end. Join to beg ch 1 with a sl st.
Round 15: Ch 1, sc2tog, 1 sc into each of next 8 (9, 10) sts, sc2tog, 1 sc into each st to end. Join to beg ch 1 with a sl st—18 (20, 22) sts.
Round 16: Using color A, ch 1, sc2tog, 1 sc into each of next 7 (8, 9) sts, sc2tog, 1 sc into each st to end. Join to beg ch 1 with a sl st—16 (18, 20) sts.
Round 17: Ch 1, sc2tog, 1 sc into each of next 6 (7, 8) sts, sc2tog, 1 sc into each st to end. Join to beg ch 1 with a sl st—14 (16, 18) sts.
Round 18: Ch 1, sc2tog, 1 sc into each of next 5 (6, 7) sts, sc2tog, 1 sc into each st to end. Join to beg ch 1 with a sl st—12 (14, 16) sts.
Round 19: Ch 1, sc2tog, 1 sc into each of next 4 (5, 6) sts, sc2tog, 1 sc into each st to end. Join to beg ch 1 with a sl st—10 (12, 14) sts.

Medium and large sizes only
Round 20: Ch 1, sc2tog, 1 sc into each of next 4 (5) sts, sc2tog, 1 sc into each st to end. Join to beg ch 1 with a sl st—10 (12) sts.

Large size only

Round 21: Ch 1, sc2tog, 1 sc into each of next 4 sts, sc2tog, 1 sc into each st to end. Join to beg ch 1 with a sl st—10 sts.

All sizes

Cut yarn leaving a tail of about 8 in (20 cm), weave yarn into each of the rem sts around top of mitten and pull firmly to close the hole at the top, but not so firmly as to make the fabric pucker. Secure with a sewing st and weave in end.

Thumb

Attach color A to thumb hole.

Round 1: Ch 1, 1 sc into each st, work 8 sc around thumb opening. Join to beg ch 1 with a sl st—12 sts.

Round 2: Ch 1, 1 sc into each st. Join to beg ch 1 with a sl st.

Rep round two 1 (1, 2) more time.

Next round: Ch 1, sc2tog, 1 sc into next 4 sts, sc2tog, 1 sc into each st to end. Join to beg ch 1 with a sl st—10 sts.

Next round: Ch 1, sc2tog, 1 sc into next 3 sts, sc2tog, 1 sc into each st to end. Join to beg ch 1 with a sl st—8 sts.

Next round: Ch 1, sc2tog, 1 sc into next 2 sts, sc2tog, 1 sc into each st at end. Join to beg ch 1 with a sl st—6 sts.

Next round: Ch 1, 1 sc into each st to end. Join to beg ch 1 with a sl st. Fasten off, again leaving a tail of about 8 in (20 cm), weave yarn into each of the rem sts around top of thumb and pull firmly to close the hole at the top. Secure with a sewing st and weave in end.

Finishing

Weave in all ends. Weave several rows of shirring elastic around cuff until it is as tight as you would like it to be.

Left mitten

Work as for right mitten until the end of rnd 5.

Round 6: Using color A, ch 1, 1 sc into each of the next 18 (20, 22) sc, ch 5 to make thumbhole, skip 4 sc, 1 sc into last sc. Join to beg ch 1 with a sl st.

Round 7: Ch 1, 1 sc into each of the next 18 (20, 22) sc, 1 sc into each ch, 1 sc into last sc. Join to beg ch 1 with a sl st—24 (26, 28) sts.

Cont to work as for right mitten.

---

tips & hints

- To change yarn on the last stitch prior to needing the new yarn, work the last 2 loops of the stitch off the hook using the new yarn. Then you will be ready to work with the new yarn at the beginning of the next stitch.

bobble scarf

For maximum winter warmth and a cool look, this extra wide and chunky scarf with giant bobbles at either end is perfect. This is super quick to make with ultra-thick yarn and a large hook.

Materials
3 x 3.5 oz (100 g) balls of Big Wool from Rowan in Bohemian
L (8 mm) crochet hook

Size
One size, 52 x 8¾ in (132 x 22 cm)

Skill
Easy

Gauge
8 sts and 4½ rows to 4 in (10 cm) measured over rows of dc using L (8 mm) hook

Special abbreviation
Bobble: make a bobble by working a number of sts into the same st, and joining them at the top. In this pattern the bobble is made of 5 dc: leaving last loop of each dc on hook work 5 dc in next dc, yo and draw through all 6 loops.

Pattern
Ch 19.

Row 1: (RS), 1 dc into 4th ch from hook (count as 1 dc), 1 dc into each ch to end, turn—17 sts.

Row 2: Ch 1, 1 sc into each of first 2 dc, *work bobble into next st, 1 sc into each of next 3 dc; rep from * to last 3 sts, 1 bobble in next, 1 sc into last dc, 1 sc into top of tch, turn.

Row 3: Ch 3 (count as 1 dc in this and following rows), skip st, 1 dc into each st to end, turn.

Row 4: Ch 1, 1 sc into each of first 4 dc, *work bobble into next st, 1 sc into each of next 3 dc; rep from *, 1 sc into top of tch, turn.

Row 5: Ch 3, skip st, 1 dc into each st to end, turn.

Rep rows 2–5 twice more.
Cont to work in dc without bobbles until scarf measures 44 in (112 cm), ending with a RS row.

Work rows 4 and 5, then rows 2 and 3. Rep last 4 rows twice more.
Fasten off.

Finishing
Gently press scarf, avoiding bobbles. Weave in all ends.

tips & hints
- As the edges of the scarf will be on show, you should avoid changing yarn at the end of a row. Instead change yarn mid-row on a wrong side row. The ends can then be woven into the fabric invisibly once the scarf is completed.

froth and frills scarf

This frilled scarf in a fluffy color-changing yarn makes a wild and wonderful look for winter. Despite its unusual appearance, it is surprisingly easy to make—you simply increase the number of stitches in each round.

Materials
2 x 1.75 oz (50 g) balls of Snowflake Chunky
   Magic from Sirdar in Purple Spray
J (6 mm) crochet hook

Size
Length: 59 in (150 cm)

Skill
Easy

Gauge
Gauge is not important for this project.

Pattern
Ch 120.

Round 1: 1 sc into 2nd ch from hook, 1 sc into each ch to last ch, 2 sc into last ch, 1 sc into the unworked bottom loop of each ch, sl st in first sc—239 sts.

Round 2: 2 sc into each sc to end, sl st in first sc—478 sts.

Round 3: Ch 3, 3 dc into each sc to end, sl st to top of beg ch 3—1434 sts.

Fasten off.

tips & hints
- Working with fluffy yarn, it can sometimes be difficult to tell exactly where the stitches are. You may find it easier to feel for the stitches, rather than look for them. In this pattern it won't matter too much if you miss a stitch or work several stitches into the same stitch.

granny squares scarf

Make this striking scarf using different colored yarns in traditional granny squares, which are then sewn together and finished with a contrasting trim.

Materials
1 x 3.5 oz (100 g) ball of Nova Super Chunky from Sirdar in each of Ivory, Damson, Pine, and Taupe
K (6.5 mm) crochet hook

Size
One size, 5½ x 64 in (14 x 163 cm). You can make the scarf longer simply by adding more squares.

Skill
Medium

Gauge
Gauge is not too important for this project.
Each square is approximately 5 in (13 cm) square.

Pattern
Make 12 squares using different combinations of colors. For maximum contrast keep back one of the colors in round 3 and use this as your border color.

Using color A, ch 6, join into a ring with a sl st.
Round 1: Ch 3 (count as 1 dc), 2 dc into ring, ch 1, work (3 dc into ring, ch 1) 3 times, sl st in top of beg ch 3.
Fasten off—12 sts.
Round 2: Join color B to same place as sl st, ch 3 (count as 1 dc), 1 dc into each of the next 2 sts. * Work (2 dc, ch 1, 2 dc) into ch-1 sp, 1 dc into each of next 3 sts; rep from * twice more, work (2 dc, ch 1, 2 dc) into last ch-1 sp, sl st into top of beg ch 3.
Fasten off—28 sts.
Round 3: Join color C to same place as sl st, ch 3 (count as 1 dc), 1 dc into each of next 4 sts * work (2 dc, ch 1, 2 dc) into ch-1 sp, 1 dc into each of next 7 sts; rep from * twice more, work (2 dc, ch 1, 2 dc) into last ch-1 sp, 1 dc into each of next 2 sts, sl st in top of beg ch 3—44 sts.
Fasten off.

Finishing
Press each square. Using color D join the squares by inserting the needle under the first st on one side of the first square and under the corresponding st on the square you are joining to. Cont to work this way from right to left until the 2 squares are completely joined along one side.

When all of the squares have been joined in this way, join color D anywhere along the scarf edge. Ch 1, work 1 sc into each st along the edges of the scarf and 3 sc in the ch-1 sp at each corner. Sl st to beg ch 1.
Fasten off. Weave in all ends.

beads and tassels scarf

Here is an elegant evening scarf made using a fine slinky yarn with beads crocheted into the fabric in a striking motif. The scarf is finished off with long beaded tassels.

Materials
1 x 1.75 oz (50 g) ball of Silky 5 Count from Twilleys in Black
C (2.75 mm) crochet hook
216 (25 g) clear beads (ensure the hole is large enough to pass a threaded needle though)

Size
One size, 33 in (84 cm) excluding fringe

Skill
Intermediate

Gauge
26 sts and 26 rows to 4 in (10 cm) measured over rows of sc using C (2.75 mm) hook

Special abbreviation
sc with bead: to work a bead into the fabric, insert hook into next st, move bead up yarn so it is close to the fabric, yo, draw through a loop, yo, draw through 2 loops on hook.

Pattern
Thread 216 beads onto the yarn. You should thread all the beads you need (and a few more in case you have miscounted) as you will not be able to add more beads unless you break the yarn. Any spare beads can be discarded at the end.

Ch 18.
Row 1: 1 sc into 2nd ch from hook, 1 sc into each ch to end, turn—17 sts.
Row 2: Ch 1, 1 sc into each sc to end, turn.
Work 3 more rows of sc.
Row 6: Ch 3 (count as 1 dc on this and following rows), skip first sc, 1 dc into each sc to end, turn.
Row 7: Ch 3, skip first dc, 1 dc into each dc to end, including tch, turn.
Row 8: Ch 3, skip first dc, 1 dc into each dc to end, including tch, turn.
Row 9: Ch 1, 1 sc into each dc to end, including tch, turn.
Row 10: Ch 1, 1 sc into each of first 7 sc, 1 sc with bead into the next 3 sc, 1 sc into each of the next 7 sc, turn.
Row 11: Ch 1, 1 sc into each sc to end, turn.
Row 12: Ch 1, 1 sc into each of first 5 sc, 1 sc with bead into the next 3 sc, 1 sc into next sc, 1 sc with bead into the next 3 sc, 1 sc into each of the next 5 sc, turn.
Row 13: Ch 1, 1 sc into each sc to end, turn.
Row 14: Ch 1, 1 sc into each of first 3 sc, 1 sc with bead into the next 3 sc, 1 sc into each of next 5 sc, 1 sc with bead into the next 3 sc, 1 sc into the last 3 sc, turn.
Row 15: Ch 1, 1 sc into each sc to end, turn.
Row 16: Ch 1, 1 sc into each of first 5 sc, 1 sc with bead into the next 3 sc, 1 sc into next sc, 1 sc with bead into the next 3 sc, 1 sc into each of the next 5 sc, turn.

Row 17: Ch 1, 1 sc into each sc to end, turn.
Row 18: Ch 1, 1 sc into each of first 7 sc, 1 sc with bead into the next 3 sc, 1 sc into each of the next 7 sc, turn.
Row 19: Ch 1, 1 sc into each sc to end, turn.
Rows 20–22: Work as rows 6–8.
Row 23: Ch 1, 1 sc into each dc to end, including tch, turn.
Rows 24–25: Ch 1, 1 sc into each sc to end, turn.
Row 26: Ch 1, 1 sc into each of first 6 sc, 1 sc with bead into each of next 5 sc, 1 sc into each of last 6 sc, turn.
Rows 27–29: Ch 1, 1 sc into each sc to end, turn.
Rep rows 6–29 seven times.
Rep rows 6–22 once more.
Work 5 rows of sc. Fasten off.

Finishing
Tassels
Cut 34 pieces of yarn of equal length. To make 1 tassel, tie a knot in an end of the yarn (or a double knot depending on how large the beads are), thread 4 beads onto each tassel. Tie a knot at the other end. Fold yarn in half. Using your crochet hook, pull the center of the yarn through the first stitch on 1 short end of scarf, ensuring that you have 2 beads on each thread and that the threads are of equal length. Pull both ends through the loop you have just made and pull firm. Cont to place 1 tassel in each st. Rep for opposite end of scarf. Press scarf, carefully avoiding beads. Weave in all ends.

basic round bag

This basic bulb bag is very straightforward and can be whipped off in an hour or two. Once you can make this, there is no end to the variations of bag you can make using different yarns, beads, tassels, loops, and textured stitches, some of which are featured later in this book.

Materials
1 x 3.5 oz (100 g) ball of Ribbon Twist from Rowan
   in Racy
L (8.00 mm) crochet hook

Skill
Easy

Gauge
Gauge is not important for this project.

Special abbreviations
sc2tog: insert hook into next st, yo, draw through the work, insert hook in next st, yo and draw through the work, yo and draw through all 3 loops, leaving just 1 loop.

Pattern
Ch 4, join into a ring with a sl st.
Round 1: Work 8 sc into the ring.
Round 2: Work 2 sc into each st—16 sts.
Round 3: *1 sc into next st, 2 sc into next st; rep from * to end—24 sts.

Cont to expand the base of the bag by increasing the number of sts between each inc by one. For example, for round 4 *1 dc into each of next 2 sts, 2 dc into next st; rep from * to end—32 sts. While you cont to inc the same number of sts in each round, the base will remain flat. Stop increasing, and the bag grows upward. To create a curve in the bottom of the base, intersperse rows of

increases with rounds of straight sc. Alternatively you could dec by only a small number of sts per sc.

If you are using a very chunky yarn, as we are here, the base will grow very quickly so at this point we slow down the rate of inc:

Round 4: 1 sc into each sc to end.
Round 5: *1 sc into each of next 2 sts, 2 sc into next st; rep from * to end—32 sts.
Round 6: 1 sc into each sc to end.
Round 7: Inc by only 4 sts in this round: *1 sc into each of next 7 sts, 2 sc into next st; rep from * to end—36 sts.

When the base is as wide as you want it, about 4 in (10 cm) in diameter, carry on crocheting 1 sc in each sc without increasing. Cont until the bag is almost as tall as you want it, say 4 in (10 cm) high, then to make the top narrower, dec 2 or 3 sts evenly over the next few rows—make sure you can still get your hand in it though!

Rounds 8–11: 1 sc into each sc to end.
Round 12: Dec by 4 sts in this round: *1 sc into each of next 7 sts, sc2tog; rep from * to end—32 sts.
Round 13: *1 sc into each of next 6 sts, sc2tog; rep from * to end—28 sts.
Round 14: *1 sc into each of next 5 sts, sc2tog; rep from * to end—24 sts.
Round 15: 1 sc into each sc to end.

Round 16: *1 sc into each of next 4 sts, sc2tog; rep from * to end—20 sts.
Rounds 17–20: 1 sc into each sc to end. Sl st into first sc. Do not fasten off.

Strap
You can use almost anything as a strap: a piece of ribbon, a silver chain, or crochet a strap. To do this, the simplest method is to make a double strap.

One sc into next st along the edge of the bag, *insert hook under left loop of the stitch you've just made, yo and draw through a loop, yo, draw through 2 loops; rep from * until strap is desired length. Attach to opposite side of bag with a sc2tog.
Fasten off.

---

tips & hints
- Although you can work in rounds that finish with a slip stitch into the first stitch of that round, it is quicker to work in a spiral, although this may be less accurate.
- When building the base, if the fabric seems to buckle or become wavy, it is likely that you are working with too many stitches. Start off with fewer stitches and increase by the same amount.

beaded evening bag

This elegant evening bag in a midnight blue shimmery yarn has a flat base and an interesting shell design, and is trimmed with a beaded edging. To finish off, a matching ribbon is threaded through the top to close.

Materials
2 balls of Lurex Shimmer from Rowan in Midnight Blue
E (3.5 mm) crochet hook
5 g (28 beads) of black seed beads (ensure the hole is large enough to pass a threaded needle through)
1 yd (1 m) of ½ in (1 cm) width dark blue velvet ribbon

Skill
Medium

Gauge
20 sts and 12 rows to 4 in (10 cm) measured over rounds of dc using E (3.5 mm) hook

Special abbreviation
sc with bead: to work a bead into the fabric, insert hook into next st, move bead up yarn so it is close to the fabric, yo, draw through a loop, yo, draw through 2 loops.

Pattern—base
Ch 6, join into a ring with a sl st.
Round 1: Work 12 sc into the ring, sl st in first sc.
Round 2: Ch 3 (count as 1 dc in this and following rounds), 1 dc into same place as sl st, 2 dc into each sc, sl st to top of beg ch 3—24 sts.
Round 3: Ch 3, 2 dc into next dc, *1 dc into next dc, 2 dc into next dc; rep from * to end, sl st in top of beg ch 3—36 sts.
Round 4: Ch 3, 1 dc into next dc, 2 dc into next dc, *1 dc into each of next 2 dc, 2 dc into next dc; rep from * to end, sl st in top of beg ch 3—48 sts.

Round 5: Ch 3, 1 dc into each of next 2 dc, 2 dc into next dc, *1 dc into each of next 3 dc, 2 dc into next dc; rep from * to end, sl st in top of beg ch 3—60 sts.
Round 6: Ch 3, 1 dc into each of next 3 dc, 2 dc in next dc, *1 dc into each of next 4 dc, 2 dc into next dc; rep from * to end, sl st in top of beg ch 3—72 sts.
Round 7: Ch 3, 1 dc into each of next 4 dc, 2 dc into next dc, *1 dc into each of next 5 dc, 2 dc into next dc; rep from * to end, sl st in top of beg ch 3—84 sts.

Shell pattern
Round 8: 1 sc into each of first 3 sts, *ch 3, skip 3 dc, 1 sc in each of next 3 dc; rep from *, ch 3, skip last 3 dc, sl st in first sc.
Round 9: *1 sc into center sc of 3 sc, 5 dc into ch-3 sp; rep from *, sl st in first sc.
Round 10: Sl st into first dc, *1 sc into each of center 3 dc, ch-3, rep from *, sl st in first sc.
Rep rounds 9 and 10 until bag measures 6 in (15 cm) high, ending with round 9.
Fasten off.

Beaded edging
Thread beads onto the yarn. It is better to thread on more than you think you will need, any extra need not be used, but if you find you don't have enough, you will need to cut the yarn and thread on more beads. Rejoin yarn where you fastened off, but work with WS facing so that the beads are on the outside of the bag.

Next round: *1 sc into of each of next 5 dc, 1 sc with bead into next sc; rep from * to end, sl st in first sc.
Next round: 1 sc into each of first 2 sc, *1 sc with bead into next sc, 1 sc into each of next 5 sc; rep from * ending 1 sc with bead into next sc, 1 sc into last 3 sc, sl st in first sc. Do not fasten off.

Strap
1 sc into next st, *insert hook under left loop of last sc, yo and draw through a loop, yo, draw through 2 loops; rep from * until strap is desired length. Attach to opposite side of bag with a sc2tog. Fasten off.

Finishing
Thread the ribbon all the way around the top of the bag through the holes in the pattern and tie with a bow.

---

tips & hints
- If you can't find a needle with a small enough head to pass through the beads, dab some glue onto the end of the yarn. Once it has hardened, you will be able to thread the beads directly onto the yarn.
- To stop the ribbon from fraying, carefully coat the ends with clear nail polish.

disco bag

Here is an amazing loop-covered bag in an interesting bobble yarn, made in spiral rounds to create a ball shape and finished off using a pearl bead necklace as a strap.

Materials
1 x 1.75 oz (50 g) ball of Domino from Sirdar in Blue
G/6 (4 mm) crochet hook
Shirring elastic
Pearl bead necklace

Skill
Medium

Gauge
Gauge is not important for this project.

Special abbreviations
loop st: This is a very simple variation on sc. Hold the work and yarn as if to sc. Insert hook into work as if to sc, pick up the yarn on both sides of the loop made by your finger, and draw the 2 strands through the st, yo and draw all loops through on hook.

sc2tog: insert into next st, yo, draw through the work, insert hook into next st, yo, draw through the work, yo and draw through all 3 loops.

Pattern
Ch 4, join into a ring with a sl st.
Round 1: Work 8 sc into the ring.
Round 2: 2 sc into each st—16 sts.
Round 3: *1 loop st into next st, 2 sc into next st; rep from * to end—24 sts.
Round 4: *1 loop st into next st, 1 sc into next st, 2 sc into next st; rep from * to end—32 sts.
Round 5: *1 loop st into next st, 1 sc into next st, 1 loop st into next st, 2 sc into next st; rep from * to end—40 sts.
Round 6: *(1 loop st into next st, 1 sc into next st) twice, 2 sc into next st; rep from * to end—48 sts.
Round 7: *(1 loop st into next st, 1 sc into next st) twice, 1 loop st into next st, 2 sc into next st; rep from * to end—56 sts.
Round 8: *(1 loop st into next st, 1 sc into next st) 3 times, 2 sc into next st; rep from * to end—64 sts.
Rounds 9–18: *1 loop st into next st, 1 sc into next st; rep from * to end.
Round 19: *(1 loop st into next st, 1 sc into next st) 3 times, sc2tog; rep from * to end—56 sts.
Round 20: *1 loop st into next st, 1 sc into next st; rep from * to end.
Round 21: *(1 loop st into next st, 1 sc into next st) twice, 1 loop st into next st, sc2tog; rep from * to end—48 sts.
Rounds 22 and 23: 1 loop st into next st, 1 sc into next st; rep from * to end.
Round 24: *(1 loop st into next st, 1 sc into next st) twice, sc2tog; rep from * to end—40 sts.

Rounds 25–27: *1 loop st into next st, 1 sc into next st; rep from * to end.
Round 28: * 1 loop st into next st, 1 sc into next st, 1 loop st into next st, sc2tog; rep from * to end—32 sts.
Rounds 29–31: *1 loop st into next st, 1 sc into next st; rep from * to end.
Round 32: 1 sc into each sc to end. Join with a sl st in first sc.
Fasten off.

Note: If you want to make the bag deeper, continue to work rounds of alternating 1 loop stitch and 1 single crochet until bag reaches desired length.

Finishing
Thread shirring elastic around the top of the bag—tight enough to close it, but make sure you can still fit your hand inside.

Thread the necklace through any stitch along the brim and then into a stitch on the opposite side to make a strap.

tips & hints
- Precision is not all-important when making this bag! Don't worry if you think you might have missed the odd stitch or added too many—this will not affect the overall shape of the bag and the loop surface will conceal any errors.

purse on a belt

Make this funky hipster belt with a wave pattern in contrasting colors, which can be worn with a matching purse that simply slides onto it.

Materials
1 x 1.75 oz (50 g) ball of Cotton Glace from Rowan in Poppy (color A)
1 x 1.75 oz (50 g) ball of Cotton Glace from Rowan in Bubbles (color B)
G/6 (4 mm) crochet hook
Large hook and eye
Snap

Belt size
Small: 29 in (74 cm)
Medium: 32 in (81cm)
Large: 35 in (89 cm)
Instructions for small size are given first. Larger sizes are in parentheses.

Skill
Medium

Gauge
18 sts and 22 rows to 4 in (10 cm) measured over rows of sc using G/6 (4 mm) hook

Special abbreviations
tr: triple crochet. Yo twice, insert the hook into next st, yo, draw through a loop, yo, draw through first 2 loops, yo, draw through next 2 loops, yo, draw through last 2 loops.

sc2tog: insert hook into next st, yo, draw through the work, insert hook into next st, yo, draw through the work, yo and draw through all 3 loops.

sc3tog: insert hook into next st, yo, draw through the work, insert hook into next st, yo, draw through the work, insert hook into next st, yo, draw through a loop, yo, draw through all 4 loops.

Pattern—belt
Using color A, ch 128 (142, 156).
Row 1: Skip 2 ch, (count as 1 sc) *1 sc into next st, 1 hdc into each of next 2 sts, 1 dc into each of next 2 sts, 1 tr into each of next 3 sts, 1 dc into each of next 2 sts, 1 hdc into each of next 2 sts, 1 sc into each of next 2 sts; rep from * to end, turn.
Row 2: Ch 1 (counts as 1 sc), skip first sc, 1 sc into each st to end including top of tch, turn.
Row 3: Change to color B, ch 4 (count as 1 tr), skip first st, *1 tr into next st, 1 dc into each of next 2 sts, 1 hdc into each of next 2 sts, 1 sc into each of next 3 sts, 1 hdc into each of next 2 sts, 1 dc into each of next 2 sts, 1 tr into each of next 2 sts; rep from * to end including top of tch.
Row 4: As row 2.
Row 5: Change to color A, ch 1 (count as 1 sc), skip first st, *1 sc into next st, 1 hdc into each of next 2 sts, 1 dc into each of next 2 sts, 1 tr into each of next 3 sts, 1 dc into each of next 2 sts, 1 hdc into each of next 2 sts, 1 sc into each of next 2 sts; rep from * to end including top of tch, turn.
Row 6: As row 2.

Finishing
Press the belt gently. Attach hook and eye to either end. Sew these in place or use crochet sl st worked into the hook and eye. Weave in all ends.

Purse
Set aside a small quantity of color A at the beginning to make the belt attachment.
Using color A, ch 22.
Row 1: 1 sc into 2nd ch from hook, 1 sc into each ch to end, turn—21 sts.
Row 2: Ch 1, 1 sc into each sc to end, turn.
Cont to work in sc for 27 more rows.
Row 30: Ch 1, 1 sc into each of next 7 sc, turn.
Working in only these 7 sts, work 5 more rows of sc. Do not fasten off. Drop loop from hook placing loop onto a safety pin so as not to unravel.
Using the yarn you set aside, rejoin yarn to the 8th st in row 29. Work 1 sc into each of next 7 sts. Working only in these 7 sts, work 5 more rows of sc.
Fasten off.
Rejoin yarn to the 15th st in row 29. Work 1 sc into each of last 7 sts.
Working only in these 7 sts, work 5 more rows of sc.
Fasten off.
Row 36: Pick up dropped loop at row 36, ch 1, work 7 sc across section, 7 sc across center section, 7 sc across side section, turn—21 dc.
Work 4 more rows of sc.
Next row: Change to color B, sc2tog, 1 sc into each sc to last 2 sts, sc2tog.
Cont to dec 1 st at each end of each row until 3 sts remain.
Next row: Sc3tog. Fasten off.

Finishing
Gently press the purse. Using sl st sew up side seams. Attach snap to flap of purse. Weave in ends.

beach tote

This sling-strapped beach tote is made from super chunky denim yarn and is tremendously quick to crochet in tall, open, double crochet stitches. It is big enough to carry everything you need for a day lounging on the beach.

Materials
3 x (3.5 oz) 100 g balls of Denim Ultra from Sirdar in Denim Blue
L (8 mm) crochet hook

Size
One size

Skill
Easy

Gauge
6½ sts and 4½ rows to 4 in (10 cm) measured over rows of dc using an L (8 mm) hook

Special abbreviation
dc2tog: yo, insert hook into next st, yo, draw loop through the work, yo, draw through 2 loops on hook (leaving 2 loops), yo, insert hook into next st, yo, draw loop through the work, yo and draw through 2 loops, yo and draw through rem 3 loops.

Pattern
Ch 4 and join into a ring with a sl st.
Round 1: Ch 3 (count as dc in this and following rnds), 11 dc into the ring, sl st in top of beg ch 3—12 sts.
Round 2: Ch 3, 1 dc into same place as sl st, 2 dc into each st, sl st in top of beg ch 3—24 sts.
Round 3: Ch 3, 1 dc into same place as sl st, *1 dc into next st, 2 dc in next st; rep from * 1 dc into last st, sl st in top of beg ch 3—36 sts.

Round 4: Ch 3, 1 dc into same place as sl st, *1 dc into each of next 2 sts, 2 dc into next st; rep from *, 1 dc into each of last 2 sts, sl st in top of beg ch 3—48 sts.
Round 5: Ch 3, 1 dc into same place as sl st, *1 dc into each of next 3 sts, 2 dc into next st; rep from *, 1 dc into each of last 3 sts, sl st in top of beg ch 3—60 sts.
Round 6: Ch 3, 1 dc into fl only of each dc to end, sl st in top of beg ch 3.
Rounds 7–10: Ch 3, 1 dc into each dc to end, sl st in top of beg ch 3.
Round 11: Ch 3, 1 dc into each of next 7 dc, dc2tog, *1 dc into each of next 8 dc, dc2tog; rep from * to end of round, sl st in top of beg ch 3—54 sts.
Round 12: Ch 3, 1 dc into each of next 6 dc, dc2tog, *1 dc into each of next 7 dc, dc2tog; rep from * to end of round, sl st in top of beg ch 3—48 sts.
Round 13: Ch 3, 1 dc into each of next 5 dc, dc2tog, *1 dc into each of next 6 dc, dc2tog; rep from * to end of round, sl st in top of beg ch 3—42 sts.
Round 14: Ch 3, 1 dc into each of next 4 dc, dc2tog, *1 dc into each of next 5 dc, dc2tog; rep from * to end of round, sl st in top of beg ch 3—36 sts.
Rounds 15 and 16: Ch 3, 1 dc into each st to end, sl st in top of beg ch 3.

Strap—side 1
Row 17: Ch 3, dc2tog, 1 dc into each of next 6 dc, dc2tog. Turn, leaving rem sts unworked. (9 sts)
Row 18: Ch 3, skip first st, 1 dc into each of next 5 dc, dc2tog, turn. (7 sts)
Row 19: Ch 3, skip first st, 1 dc into each of next 3 dc, dc2tog, turn. (5 sts)
Rows 20–32: Ch 3, skip first st, 1 dc into each of next 3 dc, 1 dc into top of beg ch 3.
Fasten off.

Strap—side 2
Skip 7 dc from last st worked on row 17, rejoin yarn in next st.
Rep rows 17–32.
Fasten off.

Finishing
With wrong side facing, sew ends of the strap together. Weave in all ends.

swirl bag

This super-fluffy and variegated yarn makes an amazing, textured fabric when crocheted. The bag is worked in a spiral covered in swirls of surface crochet for a truly eye-catching accessory!

Materials
2 x 3.5 oz (100 g) balls of Snowflake Chunky Magic from Sirdar in Raspberry Spray
J (6 mm) crochet hook
1 yd (1 m) of ½ in (1 cm) wide pink ribbon

Skill
Medium

Gauge
The gauge is not important for this project.

Special abbreviation
sc2tog: insert hook into next st, yo, draw through the work, insert hook into next st, yo and draw through the work, yo and draw through all 3 loops.

Pattern
Ch 4, join in a ring with a sl st.
Round 1: Work 8 sc into the ring—8 sts.
Round 2: 2 sc into each sc—16 sts.
Round 3: *1 sc into next st, 2 sc into next st; rep from * to end—24 sts.
Round 4: *1 sc into each of next 2 sts, 2 sc into next st; rep from * to end—32 sts.
Round 5: *1 sc into each of next 3 sts, 2 sc into next st; rep from * to end—40 sts.
Round 6: *1 sc into each of next 4 sts, 2 sc into next st; rep from * to end—48 sts.
Round 7: 1 sc into each sc to end.
Round 8: *1 sc into each of next 5 sts, 2 sc into next st; rep from * to end—56 sts.
Rounds 9–12: 1 sc into each sc to end.

Round 13: *1 sc into each of next 5 sts, sc2tog; rep from * to end—48 sts.
Round 14: 1 sc into each sc to end.
Round 15: *1 sc into each of next 4 sts, sc2tog; rep from * to end—40 sts.
Rounds 16 and 17: 1 sc into each sc to end.
Round 18: *1 sc into each of next 3 sts, sc2tog; rep from * to end—32 sts.
Rounds 19 and 20: 1 sc in each sc to end.
Do not fasten off.
Round 21: *1 sc into each of next 2 sc, sc2tog; rep from * to end—24 sts.
Rounds 22 and 23: 1 sc in each sc to end.

Surface swirls
To create the amazing whorls and swirls, you will be crocheting onto the surface of the bag. There is no exact science to this and every bag will be unique.

Swirl
Once you have completed the basic bag, insert your hook into any st in the row below the brim and make 1 sc.
Row 1: Work toward the bottom of the bag, creating a wavy line by crocheting 1 sc into the st above or to the left or right in the row below. When you reach the bottom, make a wide turn and work back toward the brim, sl st into any sc along the brim, turn.
Row 2: Ch 1, 2 sc into each sc, sl st into last sc, turn.
Row 3: Ch 1, 2 sc into each sc, sl st into last sc. Fasten off.
Rep the swirl twice more so that the swirls cover the surface of the bag more or less evenly.

Finishing
Weave in all ends. To make the strap, attach a length of ribbon to either side of the bag opening.

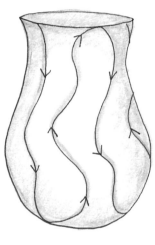

tips & hints
- When using a fluffy yarn, it can sometimes be tricky to tell exactly where the stitch is. Don't worry! As long as you keep roughly to the pattern, the bag will work out all right. Unlike knitting, you can't drop a stitch, so you won't be able to leave a hole.

gold sparkly belt

This belt using glitzy metallic yarn is the perfect way to jazz up a pair of jeans. It's made with a combination of filet and solid fabric to create an interesting stripy pattern. Make it long and wear it around the hips, or make it short for a close-fitting, waist-cinching look.

Materials
1 x 1.75 oz (50 g) ball of metallic fingering yarn in gold
D (3.25 mm) crochet hook
2 large hooks and eyes

Size
Make to any length.

Skill
Medium

Gauge
22 sts and 11 rows to 4 in (10 cm) measured over rows of dc using D (3.25 mm) hook

Pattern
Ch 10.

Row 1: 1 sc into 2nd ch from hook, 1 sc in each ch to end, turn—9 sts.

Row 2: Ch 1, 2 sc in first sc, 1 sc into each sc to last sc, work 2 sc into last sc, turn—11 sts.

Rows 3–6: Rep row 2 until you have 19 sts, turn.

Row 7: Ch 4 (count as 1 dc and 1 ch on this and following rows), skip 2 sc, 1 dc into next sc, *ch 1, skip 1 sc, 1 dc in next sc; rep from * to end, turn.

Row 8: Ch 4, skip 1 ch, 1 dc into next dc, *ch 1, skip 1 ch, 1 dc in next dc; rep from * to end, working last dc into 3rd ch of beg ch 4, turn.

Rows 9–12: Rep row 8.

Row 13: Ch 3 (count as dc in this and following rows), 1 dc into each ch and dc to end, working 1 dc into 3rd ch of beg ch 4, turn.

Rows 14 and 15: Ch 3, skip first dc, 1 dc into each dc to end, working 1 dc into top of ch of beg ch 3, turn.

Row 16: Ch 4, skip 2 dc, 1 dc into next dc, *ch 1, skip 1 dc, 1 dc into next dc; rep from * to end, working last dc into top ch of beg ch 3, turn.

Rep rows 8 to 16 until belt is 4 in (10 cm) shorter than desired length, ending with a 12th row. This allows for the remaining rows, plus the fastener. Bear in mind the fabric will have a little stretch but not much.

Next row: Ch 1, 1 sc into each dc and each ch space, turn—19 sts.

Next row: Sc2tog, work 1 sc into each sc to last 2 sts, sc2tog, turn.

Rep the last row 4 more times.

Fasten off.

Finishing
Work 2 sc into each row along length of belt, *crochet base of "eye" to end of belt by inserting hook through sc, then through base of "eye" and working 1 sc; rep from * along end, 2 sc into each row along length of belt, then crochet base of "hook" to the other end of belt.

Fasten off.

Gently press the belt.

flower hipster belt

Relive the sexy 1970s with this cool hipster belt of funky flower motifs in rainbow colors. The flowers are made individually and then sewn together. It looks perfect worn with a pair of jeans.

Materials
1 x 1.75 oz (50 g) ball of Cotton Glace from
   Rowan in each of the following colors: Poppy,
   Spice, Shoot, Bubble, and Sunny
G/6 (4 mm) crochet hook
Large hook and eye

Size
Small: 26 in (66 cm)
Medium: 30 in (76 cm)
Large: 34 in (86 cm)

Skill
Easy

Gauge
Gauge is not too important for this project. Each flower should be approximately 4 in (10 cm) in diameter.

Pattern
Make 6 (7, 8) flowers in different colors.

Ch 6, join in a ring with a sl st.
Round 1: Ch 3 (count as 1 dc), 17 dc into ring, sl st to top of beg ch 3.
Round 2: Ch 1, 1 sc into same place as sl st, *ch 3, skip 2 sts, 1 sc into next st; rep from * 5 more times, omitting last sc, sl st into first sc.
Round 3: Ch 1, *work (1 sc, 1 hdc, 3 dc, 1 hdc, 1 sc) into ch-3 sp, sl st into next sc; rep from * 5 more times.
Round 4: Sl st into each of next 4 sts, ch 1, 1 sc into same place as last sl st made, *ch 7, 1 sc into center

dc of 3 dc; rep from * 5 more times, omitting last sc of prev round, sl st to first sc this round.
Round 5: Ch 1, *work (1 sc, 2 hdc, 5 dc, 2 hdc, 1 sc) into next ch-7 sp; rep from * 5 more times, sl st into first sc.
Round 6: Ch 1, 1 sc into each st, sl st to first sc. Fasten off.

Finishing
Lay flowers with wrong side facing, and join with 2 sl sts at the top of one petal on one flower to the top of another petal on the next flower. Sew the hook onto the last flower at one end of belt, then sew eye onto the last flower at other end of belt. Weave in all ends. Press belt gently.

tips & hints
- If you want to make the flowers extra firm, you can spray a little starch onto the back.

wrist cuff and choker

This funky, metallic-style wrist cuff and choker with a checkerboard pattern is super quick to make. One ball will make dozens of cuffs or chokers, so you can make them for all your friends!

Materials
1 ball of size 5 cotton crochet yarn
C (2.75 mm) crochet hook
2 snaps for each cuff or choker

Size
One size fits all

Skill
Easy

Gauge
Gauge is not important for this project

Pattern
Ch 11.

Row 1: 1 sc into 2nd ch from hook, 1 sc into each ch to end, turn—10 sts.
Row 2: Ch 1, 1 sc into each sc to end, turn.
Rep row 2 four more times.

Mesh pattern
Row 1: Ch 5 (count as 1 dc, ch 2 in this and following rows), skip 2 sc, 1 dc into each of next 2 sc, ch 2, skip 2 sc, 1 dc into each of next 2 dc, ch 2, skip 1 sc, 1 dc into last sc, turn.
Row 2: Ch 3 (count as 1 dc in this and following rows), (2 dc into ch-2 sp, ch 2, skip 2 dc) twice, 2 dc into ch-2 sp, 1 dc into center ch of ch of beg ch 5, turn.
Row 3: Ch 5, skip 3 dc, (2 dc into ch-2 sp, ch 2, skip 2 dc) twice, 1 dc into top of of beg ch 3.

Rep rows 2 and 3 until cuff measures 5½ in (14 cm) ending after row 2. If you want to make the cuff any larger than this, work a few more rows until desired length.
Next row: Ch 1, (1 sc into each of next 2 dc, 1 sc into next ch-2 sp) twice, 1 sc into next 2 dc, turn—10 sts.
Work 5 rows of sc. Do not fasten off.

Edging
Ch 1, work 1 round of sc working 1 sc into each sc row end, 2 sc into each dc row end and 1 ch at each corner.
Fasten off.

Finishing
Weave in all ends. Press the cuff gently. Sew snaps onto each end.

Matching choker
Why not make a matching choker in the same or a different sparkly color? The pattern is identical but a little wider.

Ch 15.
Row 1: 1 sc into 2nd ch from hook, 1 sc into each ch to end, turn—14 sts.
Row 2: Ch 1, 1 sc into each sc to end, turn.
Rep row 2 four more times.

Mesh pattern
Row 1: Ch 5 (count as 1 dc, ch 2 in this and following rows), skip 2 sc, (1 dc into each of next 2 sc, ch 2, skip 2 sc) twice, 1 dc into each of next 2 sdc, ch 2, skip 1 sc, 1 dc into last sc, turn.
Row 2: Ch 3 (count as 1 dc in this and following rows), (2 dc into ch-2 sp, ch 2, skip 2 dc) 3 times, 2 dc into ch-2 sp, 1 dc into 3rd ch of beg ch 5, turn.
Row 3: Ch 5, skip 3 dc, (2 dc into ch-2 sp, ch 2, skip 2 dc) 3 times, 1 dc into top of beg ch 3.

Rep rows 2 and 3 until the choker measures 12 in (30 cm) ending after row 2. You may need to make the choker smaller or larger. Measure your neck and work choker until desired length. The length to the end of the mesh patt should be exactly the same as your neck measurement.
Next row: Ch 1, (1 sc into each of next 2 dc, 1 sc into each of next ch-2 sp) 3 times, 1 sc into next 2 dc, turn.
Work 5 rows of sc.
Fasten off.

Edging
Ch 1, work 1 round of sc, working 1 sc into each sc row end, 2 sc into each dc row end and 1 ch at each corner.
Fasten off.

Finishing
Weave in all ends. Press the choker gently. Sew snaps onto each end.

stranded choker

This sparkly choker uses strands of chains in ever-increasing lengths to create a relaxed yet elegant look.

Materials
1 x 1 oz (25 g) ball of metallic fingering yarn
   in black
D (3.25 mm) crochet hook
2 small black snaps

Size
One size

Skill
Easy

Gauge
Gauge is not important for this project.

Pattern—back panel 1
Ch 13.
Row 1: 1 sc into 2nd chain from hook, 1 sc into
   each ch to end, turn—12 sts.
Row 2: Ch 1, 1 sc into each sc to end, turn.
Work 7 more rows.
Fasten off.

Make another back panel as the first, but do not
fasten off after row 9. You will now be working
strands of chains and attaching them alternately to
back panel 1 and 2:

Strand 1: Ch 60, sl st into first sc on back panel 1.
Strand 2: Sl st into next sc on back panel 1, ch 62,
   sl st into sc on back panel 2.
Strand 3: Sl st into next sc on back panel 2, ch 64,
   sl st into sc on back panel 1.

Cont in this manner, increasing the number of
chains between panels by 2 until you have worked
to the end of both panels. You should have 12
strands, the longest being 82 chains.
Fasten off.

Finishing
Gently press. Weave in all ends.
Place 2 snaps on each back panel to fasten. You
can vary the length of the choker depending on
where you place the snaps.

---

tips & hints
- Take care that the strands are not twisted
  around one another and are hanging free
  before you attach them.

beaded choker

Make this an elegant beaded choker for glamorous parties and sophisticated soirees! Crocheting with beads adds great texture and creates a striking look.

Materials
1 x 1.75 oz (50 g) ball of Silky 5 Count from Twilleys in Black
2 mm crochet hook
176 (25 g) 4 mm black beads
2 small black snaps

Size
One size

Skill
Easy

Gauge
30 sts and 35 rows to 4 in (10 cm) measured over sc using 2 mm hook

Special abbreviation
sc with bead: to work a bead into the fabric, insert the hook into the next st, move bead up the yarn so it is close to the fabric, yo, draw through a loop, yo, draw through 2 loops.

Thread 176 beads onto the yarn. Ch 16.
Row 1: 1 sc into 2nd ch from hook, 1 sc into each ch to end, turn—15 sts.
Row 2: Ch 1, 1 sc into each sc to end, turn.
Rep row 2 eight more times.
Row 11: Ch 1, 1 sc with bead into next sc, *1 sc into next sc, 1 sc with bead into next sc; rep from * to end, turn.

Row 12: Ch 4 (count as 1 tr), skip 1 sc, 1 tr into each sc to end, turn.
Row 13: Ch 1, 1 sc with bead into next tr, *1 sc into next tr, 1 sc with bead into next tr; rep from * to end including top of tch, turn.
Rep rows 12 and 13 until choker measures 12 in (30 cm) ending with a row 13.
Next row: Ch 1, 1 sc into each sc to end.
Work 9 more rows of sc.
Fasten off.

Finishing
Gently press the choker flat. Sew snaps onto both ends.

---

tips & hints
- You can adjust the length of the choker to fit you by choosing where to place the snaps. To make the choker variable lengths, add more than one set of snaps.

fingerless gloves

These sparkly fingerless gloves don't have any fiddly shapings, just a single loop
to go over your middle finger and an opening at the thumb. They are made in one
piece from the wrist to the fingers with a seam at the side.

Materials
2 x 1 oz (25 g) balls of metallic fingering yarn in
red
1 x 1 oz (25 g) ball of metallic fingering yarn in
black
D (3.25 mm) crochet hook

Size
One size—these have a little bit of stretch so they
should fit all hand sizes.

Skill
Easy

Gauge
26 sts and 14 rows to 4 in (10 cm) measured over
dc using D (3.25 mm) hook

Special abbreviation
dc2tog: yo, insert hook into next st, yo, draw loop
through the work, yo, draw through 2 loops on
hook (leaving 2 loops), yo, insert hook into next st,
yo, draw loop through the work, yo and draw
through 2 loops, yo and draw through rem 3 loops.

Pattern
Make 2.
With red, ch 40.
Row 1: 1 dc into 4th ch from hook, 1 dc into each
ch to end—38 sts.
Rows 2–4: Ch 3 (count as 1 dc in this and
following rows), skip first dc, 1 dc into each dc to
end, working last dc into top of beg ch 3.

Row 5: Ch 3, do not skip first dc, 1 dc into each dc
to second to last st, 2 dc into last dc, dc into top
of beg ch 3—40 sts.
Row 6: Ch 3, skip first dc, 1 dc into each dc to end,
work last dc into top of beg ch 3.
Rep rows 5 and 6 until you have 48 sts, ending on
a row 5.

Next row: Ch 1, sl st into each of next 8 sts, ch 3,
skip 1 dc, dc2tog, 1 dc into each of next 12 dc,
dc2tog, turn.
Next row: Ch 3, skip first dc, dc2tog twice, 1 dc
into each of next 5 dc, dc2tog twice.
Next row: Ch 3, skip first dc, dc2tog, ch 12, skip
next 4 dc, dc2tog.
Fasten off.

Finishing
Press gloves gently.

With fingerloop on top half, fold gloves in half
along the width to form pair so that seam is on the
left side for right glove and vice versa. Using a flat
seam, join first 5 rows of glove, leave next 7 rows
of glove open for thumb, join next row.

Edging
With the right side facing, attach black to the seam
at the bottom edge. Work (1 sc, ch 2) between
each dc, sl st into first sc.
Fasten off.
Weave in all ends.

wave stripe leg warmers

These short and chic leg warmers with a wave stripe pattern and ribbed cuffs can be worn with short skirts, over boots, or even with your favorite sneakers!

Materials
1 x 1 oz (25 g) ball of Bonus Toytime DK from
   Sirdar in Popsicle
1 x 1 oz (25 g) ball of Bonus Toytime DK from
   Sirdar in Aubergine
1 x 1 oz (25 g) ball of Bonus Toytime DK from
   Sirdar in Black
G/6 (4 mm) crochet hook
7 (4.5 mm) crochet hook
Shirring elastic

Size
One size

Skill
Easy

Gauge
16 sts and 13 rows to 4 in (10 cm) measured over rows of wave st using 7 (4.5 mm) hook

Special abbreviation
sc BLO: sc into the back loop only.

Pattern
Make 2 the same.

Cuff
Ch 8 in Black using G/6 (4.00 mm) hook.
Row 1: 1 sc into 2nd ch from hook, 1 sc into each ch to end, turn—7 sts.
Row 2: Ch 1, 1 sc BLO into each sc to end, turn.

Rep row 2 until there are 42 rows.

To join, fold cuff in half to form a circle, ch 1, inserting hook into the bl only sl st to base ch. Do not fasten off.

Row 1: Ch 1, 1 sc into each row end, sl st to starting ch, turn—42 sts.
Change to Aubergine and 7 (4.5 mm) hook.
Row 2: Ch 1, *1 sc, 1 hdc, 3 dc, 1 hdc, 1 sc; rep from * to end, sl st into beg ch 1.
Row 3: As row 2.
Change to Popsicle. You can carry the first yarn on the inside of the leg warmer as you will be needing it again in 2 rows time.
Row 4: Ch 3 (count as 1 dc), skip first sc, 1 hdc, 3 sc, 1 hdc, 1 tr, *1 dc, 1 hdc, 3 sc, 1 hdc, 1 dc; rep from * to end, sl st to top of beg ch 3, turn.
Row 5: As row 4.
Rep rows 2–5 three more times, rep rows 2 and 3. Fasten off.

Make another cuff as the first, this time after you have joined the side seam of the cuff, without fastening off, sl st it to the inside of the leg warmer. Fasten off.

Finishing
Sew in all ends. Weave 3 rows of shirring elastic through each cuff until they are as tight as you need.
Fasten off.

frilly mini

This is a truly frilly mini! It is made by working rows of uneven length, from one side and working to the other, to make a wrap-around hipster skirt with a wild jagged edge. A simple ribbon tie completes the look.

Materials
4 (4, 5) 1.75 oz (50 g) balls of 4-ply (fingering weight) mohair in sky blue
7 (4.5 mm) crochet hook
1 yd (1 m) of silver ribbon

Size
Small (8–10), medium (10–12), large (12–14)
Waist measurement (actual measurement of skirt)
27 (29, 31) in
69 (74, 79) cm
Instructions for small size are given first. Larger sizes are in parentheses.

Skill
Medium

Gauge
16 sts and 18 rows to 4 in (10 cm) measured over rows of sc using 7 (4.5 mm) hook

Special abbreviations
sc2tog: insert hook into next st, yo, draw through the work, insert hook into next st, yo and draw through the work, yo and draw through all 3 loops.
For a description of how to create surface crochet, see "Collars and Cuffs" on page 30.

Pattern
Ch 51 (55, 59).
Row 1: (RS) 1 sc into 2nd ch from hook, 1 sc into each ch to end, turn—50 (54, 58) sts.
Row 2: Ch 1, 2 sc into first sc, 1 sc into each sc to end, turn—51 (55, 59) sts.
Row 3: Ch 1, 1 sc into each sc to within last sc, 2 sc into last sc, turn—52 (56, 60) sts.
Rep the last 2 rows 5 (6, 7) times—62 (68, 74) sts.
Next row: Ch 1, 1 sc into each sc to end, turn.
Next row: Ch 1, 1 sc into each sc to within last sc, sc2tog, turn—61 (67, 73) sts.
Next row: Ch 1, sc2tog, 1 sc into each sc to end, turn—60 (66, 72) sts.
Rep the last 2 rows 3 (3, 4) times—54 (60, 64) sts.
Work 5 rows without shaping.

Next row: Ch 1, 2 sc into first sc, 1 sc into each sc to end, turn—55 (61, 65) sts.
Next row: Ch 1, 1 sc into each sc to within last sc, 2 sc into last sc, turn—56 (62, 66) sts.
Next row: Ch 1, 1 sc into each sc to end, turn.
Next row: Ch 1, 1 sc into each sc to within last 2 sc, sc2tog, turn—55 (61, 65) sts.
Next row: Ch 1, sc2tog, 1 sc into each sc to end, turn—54 (60, 64) sts.
Rep the last 2 rows 6 times—42 (48, 52) sts.

Next row: Ch 1, 1 sc into each sc to end, turn.
Next row: Ch 1, 2 sc into first sc, 1 sc into each sc to end, turn—43 (49, 53) sts.
Next row: Ch 1, 1 sc into each sc to within last sc, 2 sc into last sc, turn—44 (50, 54) sts.
Rep the last 2 rows 3 (3, 4) times—50 (56, 62) sts.

Work 5 (7, 7) rows of sc without shaping.
Next row: Ch 1, 1 sc into each sc to within last 2 sc, sc2tog, turn—49 (55, 61) sts.
Next row: Ch 1, sc2tog, 1 sc into each sc to end, turn—48 (54, 60) sts.
Work 2 rows of sc without shaping.
Next row: Ch 1, 1 sc into each sc to within last 2 sc, sc2tog, turn—47 (53, 59) sts.
Next row: Ch 1, sc2tog, 1 sc into each sc to end, turn—46 (52, 58) sts.
Rep the last 2 rows 3 times—40 (46, 52) sts.
Work 3 (5, 5) rows of sc without shaping.
Next row: Ch 1, 2 sc into first sc, 1 sc into each sc to end, turn—41 (47, 53) sts.
Next row: Ch 1, 1 sc into each sc to within last sc, 2 sc into last sc, turn—42 (48, 54) sts.
Work 2 rows of sc without shaping.
Next row: Ch 1, 2 sc into first sc, 1 sc into each sc to end, turn—43 (49, 55) sts.
Next row: Ch 1, 1 sc into each sc to within last sc, 2 sc into last sc, turn—44 (50, 56) sts.
Work 3 (5, 5) rows of sc without shaping.
Next row: Ch 1, 1 sc into each sc to within last 2 sc, sc2tog, turn—43 (49, 55) sts.
Next row: Ch 1, sc2tog, 1 sc into each sc to end, turn—42 (48, 54) sts.

Rep the last 2 rows once—40 (46, 52) sts.
Work 1 row of sc without shaping.
Next row: Ch 1, 2 sc into first sc, 1 sc into each sc to end, turn—41 (47, 53) sts.

Next row: Ch 1, 1 sc into each sc to within last sc, 2 sc into last sc, turn—42 (48, 54) sts.

Rep the last 2 rows 5 times—52 (58, 64) sts.

Work 3 (3, 5) rows of sc without shaping.

Next row: Ch 1, 1 sc into each sc to within last sc, sc2tog, turn—51 (57, 63) sts.

Next row: Ch 1, sc2tog, 1 sc into each sc to end, turn—50 (56, 62) sts.

Rep the last 2 rows 4 times—42 (48, 54) sts.

Work 3 rows of sc without shaping.

Next row: Ch 1, 2 sc into first sc, 1 sc into each sc to end, turn—43 (49, 55) sts.

Next row: Ch 1, 1 sc into each sc to within last sc, 2 sc into last sc, turn—44 (50, 56) sts.

Work 2 rows of sc without shaping.

Rep the last 4 rows once—46 (52, 58) sts.

Next row: Ch 1, 2 sc into first sc, 1 sc into each sc to end, turn—47 (513, 60) sts.

Next row: Ch 1, 1 sc into each sc to within last sc, 2 sc in to last sc, turn—48 (54, 60) sts.

Work 3 rows of sc without shaping.

Next row: Ch 1, 1 sc into each sc to within last 2 sc, sc2tog, turn—47 (53, 59) sts.

Next row: Ch 1, sc2tog, 1 sc into each sc to end, turn—46 (52, 58) sts.

Work 2 rows of sc without shaping.

Rep the last 4 rows once more—44 (50, 56) sts.

Work 1 more row of sc without shaping.

Next row: Ch 1, 2 sc into first sc, 1 sc into each sc to end, turn—45 (51, 57) sts.

Next row: Ch 1, 1 sc into each sc to within last sc, 2 sc into last sc, turn—46 (52, 58) sts.

Work 4 rows of sc without shaping.

Rep the last 6 rows once more. (48 (54, 60) sts)

Next row: Ch 1, 2 sc into first sc, 1 sc into each sc to end, turn—49 (55, 61) sts.

Next row: Ch 1, 1 sc into each sc to within last sc, 2 sc into last sc, turn—50 (56, 62) sts.

Work 2 (4, 4) rows of sc without shaping on 50 (56, 62) sts. Fasten off.

Edging and Frills

Work 1 row of sc all the way along the front and bottom edges of the skirt. While working your way around, add the bottom upright frills.

With right side facing, start at the top left hand side of the skirt, and work 2 sc into each sc all the way along the left hand side. When you reach the bottom, cont to work 2 sc into every row end and approximately every 10 rows work the upright frills as follows:

Using surface crochet, work 1 row of sc into each row in a wavy line, turn. (See illustration. The line doesn't need to be too wavy as subsequent rows of increasing will make each line look very frilly.)

Next row: Ch 1, work 2 sc into each sc of frill to end, turn.

Rep the last row once more.

Next row: Ch 3 (count as 1 dc), 1 dc into each sc of frill.

Cont along the bottom edge, working 2 sc into each row end until you want to place another upright frill. When you have completed the bottom edge, incorporating all the upright frills, cont to work 2 sc into each row end or sc until you reach the top right hand side of skirt.

Next row: Ch 1, work 2 sc into each sc around the edges (omitting the upright frills).

Next row: Ch 3 (count as 1 dc), 1 dc into each sc to end. Fasten off.

Waistband

With right side facing, attach yarn to right side of skirt, work sc2tog into each pair of row ends. At the same time, use surface crochet to create the detailing down from the waistband. Make it as swirly as you want (see below). Work a continuous loop, or turn when the frond is as long as you want it to be, and work 1 sc into each sc back up to the waistband. You need to arrive back at the waistband where you left it and cont working sc2tog into row ends—75 (78, 82) sts. Work 8 rows of sc. Fasten off.

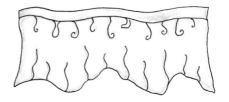

fluffy shawl

This fluffy shawl is amazingly easy to make and even easier to wear. The super fluffy yarn and open mesh pattern give this a really light feel. Wrap it around your shoulders or roll it up into a funky fluffy scarf!

Materials
3 x 1.75 oz (50 g) balls of Whisper from Patons in Black
L (8 mm) crochet hook

Size
67 x 39 in (170 x 100 cm)

Skill
Very easy

Gauge
Precise gauge is not important, but it should be quite loose.

Special abbreviation
Block—mesh hole created by ch-2 sp.

Pattern
Ch 136 very loosely.

Row 1: 1 dc into 7th ch from hook (counts as 1 dc and ch-2 sp), *ch 2, skip 2 ch, 1 dc into next ch; rep from * to end of row, turn—44 blocks.

Row 2: Ch 5 (counts as 1 dc and ch-2 sp), skip first dc, 1 dc into next dc, *ch 2, 1 dc into next dc; rep from * to within tch, turn. 1 block dec at end of row made.
Rep row 2 until just 1 block remains. Fasten off.

Finishing
Work a shell st border around the edge of the shawl as follows: *1 sc into next block, 5 dc into next block; rep from * around all 3 edges. Fasten off.

peep shoulder poncho

Crocheted in one piece so there's no sewing required, this cool poncho has cutaways at the shoulder and very simple shaping using different stitch lengths to create a long tip at the front and back. The poncho is finished with a long fringe of tassels.

Materials

5 (5, 6) x 3.5 oz (100 g) balls of Chunky Print from
    Rowan in Tart
K (6.5 mm) crochet hook
M (9 mm) crochet hook (for tassels)

Size

Small: 30–32 in (76–81 cm) bust
Medium: 34–36 in (86–91 cm) bust
Large: 38–40 in (96–102 cm) bust
Instructions for the small size are given first. Larger sizes are in parentheses.

Skill

Medium

Gauge

10 sts and 6 rows to 4 in (10 cm) measured over rows of dc using K (6.5 mm) hook

Special abbreviations

tr: triple crochet—yo twice, insert hook into work, yo, draw through work, yo, draw through first 2 loops, yo, draw through next 2 loops, yo, draw through last 2 loops.

Shell: work (2 tr, ch 2, 2 tr) into next st.

Pattern—front

Ch 62 (66, 70) for neck edge, join with a sl st to first ch, making sure you don't twist the base ch.

Round 1: Ch 1, 1 sc into each ch to end, sl st into first sc, turn—62 (66, 70) sts.
Row 2: Ch 3, (count as 1 dc in this and following rows), * 1 dc into each of next 14 (15, 16) sts, 2 dc in next st; rep from * once more, turn—33 (35, 37) sts.
Row 3: Ch 3, 1 dc in first dc, 1 dc into each st to end, 2 dc into top of beg ch 3, turn.
Rep row 3 a total of 5 (5, 6) more times until you have 45 (47, 51) sts.
Next row: Ch 3, 1 dc in first dc, 1 dc into each of next 15 (16, 18) sts, 1 tr into each of next 5 sts, skip 1 dc, work 1 shell (2 tr, ch 2, 2 tr) into next dc, skip 1 dc, 1 tr into each of next 5 sts, 1 dc into each of next 15 (16, 18) sts, work 2 dc into top of beg ch 3. Fasten off.

Back

Rejoin yarn to next st of round 1 after front.
Beg with row 2, work as front.

Joining round

Rejoin yarn to top of ch 3 at beg of last row on front, ch 3 (count as 1 dc), 1 dc into each of next 16 (17, 19) dc, 1 tr into each of next 6 tr, skip 1 tr, work 1 shell into ch-2 sp, skip 1 tr, 1 tr into each of next 6 tr, 1 dc into each of next 17 (18, 20) dc, 1 dc into top of ch 3 on back, 1 dc into each of next 16 (17, 19) dc, 1 tr into each of next 6 tr, skip 1 tr, work 1 shell into ch-2 sp, skip 1 tr, 1 tr into each of next 6 tr, 1 dc into each of next 17 (18, 20) dc, sl st to top of beg ch 3.

Next round: Ch 3, 1 dc into each of next 16 (17, 19) dc, 1 tr into each of next 7 tr, skip 1 tr, work 1 shell into ch-2 sp, skip 1 tr, 1 tr into each of next 7 tr, 1 dc into each of next 34 (36, 40) dc, 1 tr into each of next 7 tr, skip 1 tr, work 1 shell into ch-2 sp, skip 1 tr, 1 tr into each of next 7 tr, 1 dc into each of next 17 (18, 20) dc, sl st to top of beg ch 3.
Rep the last round, each time working 1 more tr either side of the shell until poncho measures 21 (22, 24) in, 53 (56, 61) cm, at center front.
Fasten off.

Finishing

Gently press poncho. Weave in all ends.

Tassels

Using a piece of card 7 in (18 cm) wide, wrap the yarn around the card. Cut the yarn down one side of the card so that you have strands. Divide the strands into bundles of four and fold the bundle in half, draw the center of the bundle through a st using the L (9 mm) hook, feed the ends through the loop, and pull tight. Place the tassels evenly all the way around the bottom edge.

sparkly halterneck

Here is a foxy, fluffy evening halterneck top that's super simple to make, using a sl:immery yarn and worked in just one piece. It ties at the neck and the waist.

Materials

2 x 3.5 oz (100 g) balls of Snowflake Chunky from Sirdar in Black Shimmer
H (5 mm) crochet hook
1 m (1 yd) of 1 cm (1/2 in) wide black velvet ribbon

Size

Small: 30–32 in (76–81 cm) bust
Medium: 32–34 in (81–86 cm) bust
Large: 34–36 in (86–91 cm) bust
Instructions for small size are given first. Larger sizes are in parentheses.

Skill

Medium

Gauge

11 dc and 12 rows to 4 in (10 cm) measured over rows of sc using H (5 mm) hook

Special abbreviation

sc2tog: insert hook into next st, yo, draw through the work, insert hook into next st, yo, draw through the work, yo, draw through all 3 loops.

Pattern

Ch 68 (72, 76).
Row 1: 1 sc into 2nd ch from hook, 1 sc into each ch to end, turn—67 (71, 75) sts.
Row 2: Ch 1, 1 sc into each sc to end, turn.

Row 3: Ch 1, sc2tog, 1 sc into each sc to last 2 sts, sc2tog, turn—65 (69, 73) sts.
Cont to dec 1 st at each end of each alternate row until 31 (35, 39) sts rem.
Work 2 rows without shaping.
Cont to dec 1 st at each end of next and every 3rd row until 23 (25, 29) sts rem.

Shape neck

Next row: Ch 1, sc2tog, 1 sc into each of next 4 sts, sc2tog, turn, leaving rem 17 (19, 21) sts unworked—6 sts.
Next row: Ch 1, sc2tog, 1 sc into each of next 2 sts, sc2tog, turn—4 sts.
Next row: Ch 1, sc2tog twice, turn—2 sts.
Next row: Ch 1, sc2tog—1 st rem.

Neck Tie

Make the tie as follows: insert hook into far left loop of sc2tog, yo and draw through a loop, yo, draw through 2 loops, *insert hook under left loop of the st you've just made, yo and draw through a loop, yo, draw through 2 loops; rep from * until strap is desired length. Fasten off.

With right side facing, rejoin yarn at edge st of last row.
Next row: Ch 1, sc2tog, 1 sc into each of next 4 sts, sc2tog, turn leaving center 11 (13, 15) neck sts unworked—6 sts.

Next row: Ch 1, sc2tog, 1 sc into each of next 2 sts, sc2tog, turn—4 sts.
Next row: Ch 1, sc2tog twice, turn—2 sts.
Next row: Ch 1, sc2tog—1 st rem.
Make another tie for other side.

Finishing

Take a length of a black ribbon and thread through bottom corners.

---

tips & hints

- Working with a fluffy yarn, especially in black, it can be quite difficult to see your stitches. Try working under a bright light and feeling for the stitches between the thumb and middle finger of your left hand.
- Take care to count your stitches regularly; fluffy wool cannot be unraveled as easily as smooth wool and mistakes may be harder to rectify.
- To stop the ribbon from fraying, coat the ends neatly with a layer of clear nail polish.

itsy-bitsy bikini

For the hottest look on the beach, what could be better than a crocheted bikini in cool cotton with a fitted top and saucy tie bottoms?!

Materials

2 x 3.5 oz (100 g) balls of Pure Cotton DK from Sirdar in Soft Green

G/6 (4 mm) crochet hook

Size

Small: 30–32 in (76–81 cm) bust
Medium: 32–34 in (81–86 cm) bust
Large: 34–36 in (86–91 cm) bust
Instructions for small size are given first. Larger sizes are in parentheses.

Skill

Medium

Gauge

17 sts and 10 rows to 4 in (10 cm) measured over rows of dc using G/6 (4 mm) hook

Special abbreviation

sc2tog: insert hook into next st, yo, draw through the work, insert hook into next st, yo, draw through the work, yo, draw through all 3 loops.

Pattern—bikini top

Ch 50 (50, 54).

Row 1: 1 sc into 2nd ch from hook, 1 sc into each ch to end, turn—49 (49, 53) sts.

Row 2: Ch 1, 1 sc into each sc to end, turn.

Small size

Row 3: As row 2.

Medium and large sizes

Row 3: Ch 1, 1 sc into each of next (11, 12) sc, 3 sc into next sc, 1 sc into each of next (25, 27) sc, 3 sc into next sc, 1 sc into each of next (11, 12) sc, turn—49 (53, 57) sts).

All sizes

Row 4: Ch 1, 1 sc into each of next 11 (12, 13) sc, 3 sc into next sc, 1 sc into each of next 25 (27, 29) sc, 3 sc into next sc, 1 sc into each of next 11 (12, 13) sc, turn—53 (57, 61) sts.

Row 5: Sl st across first 4 sts, 1 sc into each of next 2 sts, 1 hdc into next st, 1 dc into each of next 5 (6, 7) sts, 3 dc into next st, 1 dc into each of next 5 (6, 7) sts, 1 hdc into next st, 1 sc into each of next 2 sts, sl st across next 11 sts, 1 sc into each of next 2 sts, 1 hdc into next st, 1 dc into each of next 5 (6, 7) sts, 3 dc into next st, 1 dc into each of next 5 (6, 7) sts, 1 hdc into next st, 1 sc into each of next 2 sts, skip last 4 sts, turn.

Row 6: Ch 1, 1 sc into each of next 2 sts, 1 hdc into next st, 1 dc into each of next 6 (7, 8) sts, 3 dc into next st, 1 dc into each of next 6 (7, 8) sts, 1 hdc into next st, 1 sc into each of next 2 sts, sl st across next 11 sts, 1 sc into each of next 2 sts, 1 hdc into next st, 1 dc into each of next 6 (7, 8) sts, 3 dc into next st, 1 dc into each of next 6 (7, 8) sts, 1 hdc into next st, 1 sc into each of next 2 sts, turn—57 (61, 65) sts.

Right cup—small and medium sizes

Row 7: Ch 1, 1 sc into each of next 2 sts, 1 hdc into next st, 1 dc into each of next 15 (17) sts, 1 hdc into next st, 1 sc into each of next 2 sts, turn—21 (23) sts.

Right cup—large size

Row 7: Ch 1, 1 sc into each of next 2 sts, 1 hdc into next st, 1 dc into each of next 9 sts, 3 dc into next st, 1 dc into each of next 9 sts, 1 hdc into next st, 1 sc into each of next 2 sts, turn—27 sts.

All sizes

Row 8: Ch 3 (count as 1 dc), 1 dc into each st to end, 1 dc into each sl st in row 5, turn.

Row 9: Ch 1, sc2tog twice, 1 sc into each of next 2 sts, 1 hdc into next st, 1 dc into each dc to end, work 1 dc into side of row 8, work 3 dc into side of row 7, skip 2 sl st, sl st into next sl st at center, turn.

Row 10: Ch 1, skip sl st, 1 sc into each of next 2 sts, 1 hdc into next st, 1 dc into each dc to last 5 (7, 5) sts, 1 hdc into next st, 1 sc into each of next 2 sts, sc2tog once (twice, once), turn.

Row 11: Ch 1, sc2tog once (twice, once), 1 sc into each of next 2 sts, 1 hdc into next st, 1 dc into each st to last 7 sts, 1 hdc into next st, 1 sc into each of next 6 sts, sl st into next sl st at center.

Row 12: Ch 1, skip sl st, 1 sc into each of next 6 sts, 1 hdc into next st, 1 dc into each st to last 5 (7, 5) sts, 1 hdc into next st, 1 sc into each of next 2 sts, sc2tog once (twice, once), turn.

Rows 13 and 14: Rep rows 11 and 12.

Large size

Rep rows 11 and 12 once, ending sl st into sc at end of row 11.

Next row: Ch 1, 1 sc into each st to 2nd to last st, sl st into last sc, turn.

All sizes

Next row: Ch 1, skip sl st, 1 sc into each sc to end, work 1 sc into each row end.

Fasten off.

Left cup

With RS facing, rejoin yarn at left side of left cup. Work left cup as right cup. Do not fasten off at the end of last row.

Shell edging

Ch 1, *skip 1 sc, work 3 dc into next sc, skip 1 sc, 1 sc into next sc; rep from * to end of left cup, sl st into center sl st, rep from * to end.

Fasten off.

Straps

Join yarn at side of bikini with 1 sc, *insert hook under left loop of the sc, yo, draw through a loop, yo, draw through 2 loops; rep from * until strap is desired length. Rep for the other side.

Join yarn at top of cup with sc2tog, turn, 1 sc into the sc2tog, turn. Work as side strap. Rep for other side.

Bottom

Starting at the front, ch 29 (33, 37).

Row 1: 1 sc into 2nd ch from hook, 1 sc into each ch to end, turn—28 (32, 36) sts.

Row 2: Ch 1, sc2tog, 1 sc into each sc to last 2 sts, sc2tog, turn—26 (30, 34) sts.

Dec 1 st at each end of every row until 18 (20, 22) sts rem.

Next row: Ch 1, 1 sc into each st to end, turn.

Next row: Dec 1 st at each end of row—16 (18, 20) sts.

Rep last 2 rows 1 (2, 3) more time(s)—14 sts.

Work 3 rows straight without shaping.

Dec 1 st at each end of next and foll 4th row—10 sts.

Work 13 rows straight without shaping.

Inc 1 st at each end of next and each foll alternate rows until you have 20 sts as follows.

Next row: Ch 1, 2 sc in first sc, 1 sc into each sc to last sc, 2 sc in last sc, turn.

Inc 1 st at each end of next 3 rows—26 sts.

Inc 1 st at each end of next and foll alternate rows until you have 48 (52, 56) sts.

Inc 1 st at each end of next 2 rows—52 (56, 60) sts.

Do not fasten off.

Shell border—back

Ch 1, * skip first sc, 3 dc into next sc, skip 1 sc, 1 sc into next sc; rep from * to end.

Fasten off.

Shell border—front

Rejoin yarn at side edge of front, ch 1, *skip first ch, 3 dc into next ch, skip 1 ch, 1 sc into next ch; rep from * to end.

Fasten off.

Ties

Follow instructions for bikini top straps to make ties for each of the 4 corners of the bikini bottom.

---

tips & hints

- For more cup allowance, place the neck ties slightly off-center, toward the outer edges of the bikini top.

index

new and bestselling titles

Martingale®
& COMPANY

America's Best-Loved Craft & Hobby Books®
America's Best-Loved Knitting Books®

crochet

Classic Crocheted Vests

Crochet for Babies and Toddlers

Crochet for Tots

Crocheted Aran Sweaters

Crocheted Lace

Crocheted Socks!

Crocheted Sweaters

**The Little Box of Crocheted Hats
and Scarves NEW!**

Today's Crochet

knitting

200 Knitted Blocks NEW!

365 Knitting Stitches a Year
Perpetual Calendar

Basically Brilliant Knits

Beyond Wool

Classic Knitted Vests

Comforts of Home

Dazzling Knits

Fair Isle Sweaters Simplified

First Knits NEW!

A Garden Stroll

Handknit Style NEW!

Knit it Now!

Knits for Children and Their Teddies

Knits from the Heart

Knitted Shawls, Stoles, and Scarves

Knitted Throws and More
for the Simply Beautiful Home

The Knitter's Book of Finishing Techniques

A Knitter's Template

Knitting with Hand-Dyed Yarns

Knitting with Novelty Yarns

Lavish Lace

The Little Box of Scarves

The Little Box of Scarves II NEW!

The Little Box of Sweaters

More Paintbox Knits

The Pleasures of Knitting NEW!

Pursenalities

Rainbow Knits for Kids NEW!

Sarah Dallas Knitting NEW!

Simply Beautiful Sweaters

Simply Beautiful Sweaters for Men

Style at Large

A Treasury of Rowan Knits

The Ultimate Knitted Tee

The Ultimate Knitter's Guide

Our books are available at bookstores and your favorite craft, fabric, and
yarn retailers. If you don't see the title you're looking for, visit us at
www.martingale-pub.com or contact us at: **1-800-426-3126**
International: 1-425-483-3313 • Fax: 1-425-486-7596 • Email: info@martingale-pub.com